Hidden Treasures in Secret Places

TULSA

ISBN: 978-1-957262-99-4
Hidden Treasures in Secret Places: How Jesus Restores Lives Through Beth Shalom

Yorkshire Publishing
1425 E 41st Pl
Tulsa, OK 74105
www.YorkshirePublishing.com
918.394.2665

Published in the USA

Hidden Treasures in Secret Places

ONE WOMAN'S STORY OF INNER HEALING AND DELIVERANCE

Monte Bromiley

I will give you hidden treasures, riches stored in secret places, so that you may know that I am the Lord, the God of Israel, who summons you by name.
Isaiah 45:3 (NIV)

Contents

Introduction

My name is Monte Bromiley. I live in a small town in Texas. I live in a big, open field with land all around me, in a blue house. I raised my children in this house, and my grandchildren now play in these same fields. I was in a difficult marriage for many years. That was hard for my children and me on so many levels, but it also taught us total dependency on the Lord, and we came to see supernatural provision and healing as regular occurrences. God was our healer, provider and protector. After many years of being on my own, I am now remarried to a wonderful man. I never set out to write a book, or have a ministry, or do anything besides raise my children, teach kindergarten, go to church, love Jesus and take care of the people around me, but in the process of loving Jesus and taking care of these people, I got pulled into a much deeper divine plan.

I always had a heart for broken and lost people. When I was young and would pray for hurting or broken people and nothing would happen, I wanted to know why. I came to the place where I told the Lord I would walk away from it all if I couldn't see that what was in the Bible is real. I grew up in church, and I grew up believing God, even though there were many things about God that the church either did not teach, or taught wrong, and unanswered questions only made me doubt. Why wasn't I seeing the healing I read about? Why were believers not free, as Jesus promised?

It was these questions that truly brought me face to face with God and started me on this journey. He had a predetermined destiny for me, and when I started asking questions and asking Him for answers, my whole life changed. He began to show me hidden treasures, secrets of His heart, so that I would know Him and be able to show Him to those around me.

I suppose I am going to try and tell you the story of Beth Shalom, of how I have come to see the face, the power, and the freedom of God every day. I will try to go in an order that makes sense. I will insert many, many scripture references, because the Word is my food and it was my teacher all throughout this process. God brought scriptures alive to me to teach and train me, and I would read them in ways I never had before. I will try to explain some of the tools I now have so that you can apply them to your own life. But mostly, I want to tell you stories of what has happened to me, and what I have seen God do all around me. I want to spark a fire in you to go after the things of God. He IS good. What he says IS true. We have ALL authority and ALL access in the Kingdom of Light. And there is a hurting, dying world, and a hurting, dying church, that needs to know they have power over the enemy, and the true promise of God's abundant life. They need to be healed.

Start asking God to teach you and train you. The Lord, the God of Israel, summons you by name. He has treasures for you, buried in deep, dark places. If you find them, you will never be the same.

A Challenge from Hell

In my early twenties I taught a Bible Study to Junior High school girls at a Christian school in Texas. One evening as I prepared for class, I felt the Lord impress on my heart and mind to teach about unforgiveness. I studied all the next day and found several passages to share, and when I got to Bible Study, I shared the scriptures the Lord had given me. The girls were attentive, and the lesson was going well. I asked them to bow their heads, close their eyes and think of people and things they might need to forgive. As we were praying, one of the girls suddenly spoke out in a deep, raspy, demonic voice that was not at all her normal sweet middle school girl voice.

"I'll never forgive," she hissed, beginning to shake. I told her that the Bible says we can and must forgive. She shook her head. "No, I can't!"

"Yes, you can."

Again, she shook her head, "No!" I'd had enough experiences to know that this was a demon.

Feeling as if I was in over my head and might need some backup, I sent two of the girls to look for one of the elders of the church. The girls returned and said no one was in the building but us. Their eyes were on me, waiting to see what I would do next.

Many people who grew up in church say there are no demons, and there are differing opinions as to whether or not Christians can even have them. Some believe that once saved, we are sealed and protected from such things, while others disagree. Now by this point, I had already started my journey of asking God to teach me how to help the people I came in contact with.

I would read in the Bible that if the Son sets us free, we will be free, indeed. Now I believed that, but I didn't understand why people who loved the Lord could struggle so much with sicknesses, patterns of sin, addictions and other things I had seen growing up, so I started asking for tools to set people free. By this time I was here, teaching these girls, I'd already begun to experience things like this: I had seen demons manifest, people in bondage, and people set free. You may hold whatever opinion you would like, but once you come face to face with the demonic, there is no denying it. This was a demon. And Jesus gave us all authority over demons.

> *When Jesus had called the Twelve together, he gave them power and authority to drive out all demons and to cure diseases (Luke 9:1, NIV).*

I told the girls to lay their hands on her and pray. "Pray in tongues if you can or pray in English. Just pray." After a few minutes of praying, the room became hot and muggy. I asked one of the girls to open the door to let some air in. Instantly, the atmosphere changed both in temperature and in feeling. The room cooled down and we knew the demon was gone. No one had to say it. Just like in the Bible, when the tormentor leaves, there is instant change. This young girl was free!

All of the young ladies began to share what they had seen and felt during the intense time of warfare and prayer. Some of them had visions. Some heard the voice of God. They were all instantly changed and marked. They'd seen into the spirit realm and watched this girl change in front of them. Where the kingdom of God is, the demons flee!

As I lay in bed that night I asked the Lord, "God, what happened? What was that?"

He said, "If you don't get her healed, the demons will come back."

That was not what I wanted to hear, because it meant the battle wasn't over. So, I went to school the next morning and took the girl out of class. Out on the playground, sitting on the swings I told her what God said, and asked her what it was she could not forgive. She began to cry and told me she had memories of horrible things happening to her as a tiny girl. As she shared with me, I knew I must lead her through forgiving each and every one of these memories. We forgave the people. We forgave the fear and the trauma she went through. We forgave how it made her feel.

And I watched God put her heart back together.

That was how God began making it very clear to me that if I wanted to see people get free, I had to use forgiveness to 'close the gates' in their souls so demons could not come back in.

> *"Then the spirit finds seven other spirits more evil than itself, and they all enter the person and live there. And so that person is worse off than before"* (Luke 11:26, NLT).

13

After that day in the little church room with all those junior high girls, word began to get out that I could expel demons. Ha! This was news to me! For years, I had loved Jesus, and would just pray for people and try to help them over the obstacles in their lives. I never set out to do this, but as I prayed and lived life with people in those early years, I realized that any obstacle can be an access point for the demonic. I also realized that all of us can exercise authority over demons, but few of us are ever trained in it.

This junior high girl was an early lesson. She had been traumatized at the age of three. That trauma became the opening, or gate, to her soul, and she had been tormented ever since. God was teaching me that the enemy of our souls must have access to bring torment to God's people. If I was going to help people grow spiritually, be able to change and be free, I would have to work to locate those access points and remove all the ground the enemy had stolen.

From that point on I started looking for these demonic gates, helping people close them for good. The Bible calls them the "Gates of Hell." It also tells us they will not prevail if we fully understand and acknowledge that Jesus is the Christ, the Son of the Living God.

> *Simon Peter replied, "You are the Christ, the Son of the living God." And Jesus answered him, "Blessed are you, Simon Bar-Jonah! For flesh and blood has not revealed this to you, but my Father who is in heaven. And I tell you, you are Peter, and on this rock, I will build my church, and the gates of hell shall not prevail against it" (Matthew 16:16-19, ESV).*

One Sunday afternoon I was in the park for a Baptism Service. There was a potluck, of course, and I grabbed a large, juicy fried chicken breast and headed to sit by the river to enjoy it. I was hungry, and fried chicken was going to hit the spot. I sat down excitedly … when I saw a woman sitting on a nearby bench. Immediately, I knew something was wrong with her. She wore ripped, dirty clothes, had matted hair, and it was easy to see she was deeply disturbed: she couldn't sit still, and, she was very jittery, looking around with jerky movements in every direction. I knew the Lord wanted me to sit beside her, but I have to be honest: I just wanted to eat my fried chicken! But I also knew I had been asking God to teach me things, so I needed to be obedient, fried chicken or not.

Then the Lord told me, "Give her your plate of food."

Oh, I wanted that fried chicken! But God wanted obedience so He could show me His power at work. I gave her my lunch and she ate as though she hadn't eaten in days. I asked her name and if she would like me to pray for her. She nodded, but said nothing. I prayed and bound the enemy, and the crazy agitation left her. She was able to speak coherently, and she began to tell me her story.

When she was seventeen, she had taken LSD at a party with a friend. She had not been normal since. She had a bad psychedelic trip and never came down. Drugs, I learned over the years, can open a gate and give the enemy access to come in and torment God's people. One drug, one time and she had lost her mind!

That experience had fractured her, and she had lived from this fragmented, broken place for over fifteen years. She became incapable of normal social interaction and, in an effort to help, her parents had taken her to several psychics and witches. This was another demonic access point for the enemy. She was put under spells and given various potions, none of which helped, but compounded her disoriented mental state. Her parents didn't know what to do. They put her in a trailer away from civilization and separated her from family and friends. Finally, she ended up living on the street.

I prayed for her and brought her to the place of peace that can only come from the Lord. We shut the gates in her soul to the enemy and opened them to Jesus. He touched her mind, healed her memories and she was completely changed. Soon she was sitting in front of me in her right mind with her sanity completely restored. It was amazing!

Several years later I ran into her in downtown San Marcos.

She said, "You're the woman who prayed for me in the park, and you gave me your fried chicken! I've been praying that I'd see you again." She had a job and a place to live but was thinking about me because she didn't know what to do about her anger. "I'm angry," she said. "I'm angry that my parents took me to psychics and witches, instead of to Jesus, and I lost fifteen years of my life!"

I told her that her parents could only give what they had, and they didn't have Jesus. God had brought her to the park that day to meet someone who could help her meet Jesus and be healed. I led her through more prayers of forgiveness. She felt peaceful.

How amazing is our God! He can take a life that has been lost and hopeless for years and turn it around in minutes. He is always looking for the one through whom He can show Himself mighty.

I remember the day years ago this Scripture awakened something inside of me:

> *For the eyes of the Lord run to and fro throughout the whole earth, to show Himself strong on behalf of those, whose heart is loyal to Him (2 Chronicles 16:8-10, NKJV).*

I put down my Bible and stood up. I waved my hands in the air and said, "Here I am!" I knew that if God's Word said, *His eyes are looking throughout the earth*, He might see me if I made enough noise!

"Use me, God! I want to see your power! You have my heart. Here I am. You don't have to look any further. I'll do whatever you want me to do." I began to use this Scripture in my prayers. "God, you are looking for people and places to show your power. Show yourself strong and use me to do it!"

That junior high girl and the woman on the bench were some of the early fruits of me asking God to use me to destroy the works of the enemy, and to seek and save the lost.

Fractures and Forgiveness

Two of the very earliest lessons God taught me in order to give me tools to set people free were about fractures and forgiveness. I grew up knowing that Jesus forgives all of our sins and nothing but the blood of Jesus has that power. But I did not know the power my own forgiveness held. The demon inside that little girl – the one swearing it would never forgive – solidified something God had already been showing me. The scriptures say that if YOU forgive a sin, it is forgiven, and if YOU do not forgive, then it is not forgiven. Some translations of the Bible say if we do not forgive a sin, it is retained. Either way, it is a very simple, very clear scripture that we may choose to believe or not.

> *If you forgive any man his sins, they are forgiven. If you do not forgive them, they are not forgiven (John 20:23, NLT).*

I thought forgiveness was about letting the other person off the hook because I have been forgiven. It is much more powerful than that, though. Demons live in unforgiveness. I have the power to forgive sin as a priest, and a power to release sin from being retained. When I forgive ANY sin, it releases it, and all of its affects, from being attached to that person.

God taught me that when we choose not to forgive, it creates an access point for the enemy to move in and take ground in our lives. Early in my journey I didn't quite understand why, but I knew it became important to forgive anything and everything I could think of, just as it became important to ask forgiveness.

For example, the junior high girl had been living with the effects of the trauma for several years. Her soul was storing the trauma and holding onto it because it had not been forgiven. Forgiveness was not about letting her abusers off the hook; it was about the fact that without forgiveness, the sin done against her and all its affects had been retained in her soul. Freedom came when she forgave the people who had abused her. She didn't only have to forgive what they had done, she also had to forgive how it made her feel. She had to forgive believing lies that she had done something wrong to deserve it. She had to forgive her parents for not protecting her, and she had to forgive God for not stopping these bad things from happening.

When we forgive, it releases the sin from being retained. It takes ground back that the enemy has been allowed to use, and it closes the door to the access point of the sin, the trauma, and the unforgiveness in our souls. Then we can get healed. When there is unforgiveness, there is no space for healing.

In Exodus, we see the Israelites instructed to apply the blood of the Lamb to both sides of the door and over the top, so that the angel of death would pass over them. I asked the Lord why He told them to put blood on both sides of the door, and on the top. He reminded me of the parable of the two men who owed a debt. The first man was forgiven a large sum of money. He left with his debt forgiven and feeling happy about it. Then, when he ran into a man who owed him a small amount of money, he chose not to forgive him and demanded the money be paid back in full. The man didn't have the money so he was thrown into jail and turned over to the tormentors. The first man was completely forgiven of his significant debt, but he refused to forgive the one who had sinned against him.

As believers, we have the responsibility to apply the blood to "both sides of the door." We need to ask forgiveness for our own sin, as well as to forgive those sins that have been passed down to us, or committed against us. When the blood of the spotless Lamb is applied to both sides of the door and to the top, the enemy can no longer gain entrance into our lives.

After we forgive, God can heal the broken places. The enemy is the enemy of our soul, which is our mind, will and emotions. Fractures are the broken places in our soul where the enemy has come in to steal, kill and destroy. Much like the rings on a tree when it is cut down, the inside of our souls register hurt, pain, sin, memories and trauma. Things shift in our souls after a fracture. You show me a broken person, and I will listen to him or her long enough to find a fracture – a part that has split, splintered, or hardened in order to make it through. God wants to heal all of those fractures and put our souls back together piece by piece. That's what was going on with the young junior high girl and the young woman at the park. When we find the fracture and forgive it, God can come in with his freedom.

I found anyone I could who wanted to dig into the things of God with me. We began a weekly Bible Study to share with each other what we were learning (we still meet to this day, after 40 years!).

Word first spread that I could 'expel demons,' then word spread that God was doing all sorts of things with this group of crazy people, then it began to circulate that we could teach people how to get free from sin, illness, and other problems. Soon, people were just showing up at Bible Study to ask for prayer.

One evening as we were about to begin, a woman walked up the steps to the front porch. I saw her though the glass on my front door and thought – *I met her at church… what is her name, Lord?* I heard the Lord answer me clearly – *Becca. Her name is Becca.*

As I opened the door, she said, "Hello. My name is Carrie. My boyfriend told me if I come here, you would pray for me and the voices in my head would stop." There was a day that if someone had said that to me, I would have explained, but by this time, I had seen God do all kinds of crazy things, so if anyone, anywhere asked me for prayer, I'd just say yes.

"I'm glad you're here, Carrie. We're having Bible study. I'd be glad to talk with you and pray for you afterward. Come on in." *God, are you setting me up? You said her name was Becca!*

After Bible Study I heard her story. I learned that her boyfriend had seen a demon in her. "Go get this lady to pray for you, or we're done," he'd told her, so here she was. As I continued to hear her story, I realized that Carrie was my first truly divided person.

I have since ministered to many kids like this. They were abused by their parents or someone else, and now they are broken. Then the parents ship them off and justify it by saying, "Oh, she has an eating disorder" – (or anxiety issues, or ADHD) "– she needs to be where they can really help her and monitor her."

Except, they almost never need that. They need to be with parents who love them. They need to be safe from abuse. They need to be where someone will lovingly tend to the hurt and the trauma, and love them back to wholeness. They need healing . . . they need Jesus.

Now I found myself ministering to my first full-blown multiple personality in my early thirties. I knew all the prayers and I knew all the scriptures and how to cast out devils, but I did not yet know how to access the broken places of the soul. This girl needed healing in the broken parts of her soul, and just casting out devils was not going to put her back together and heal her broken heart. I had never learned how to do this in any church I'd ever been to.

That first night Carrie came to Bible Study, a few leaders and I went upstairs to pray with her. Before I could even say a word, the devil in her came at me with profanity, telling me all kinds of vile things. At that point, something holy rose up in me. It wasn't me. It must have been the Lord because out of my mouth came, "You will not speak to me like that in my own home."

And the authority in that voice silenced the demon. I didn't say, "In the name of Jesus." I didn't say any of the things I was getting ready to say. Something I had never felt before had risen up, and out of my mouth came a quiet but firm authority that brought everyone to attention, including me.

The demon sat straight up in that little girl, looked me straight in the eyes and said, "Who are you?"

"I am an apostle of the Most High God, and you will not speak to me like that." Bam! It was over just like that. I had never seen anything like it, nor had my friends. We were all shocked. Carrie calmed, and I began to talk to her.

"What's going on that you have this kind of torment in your life?"

She wept and wept, eventually telling us her story. This girl had been thrown away. She'd been broken and sent away, with no home and no family. Now, when the boyfriend threatened to throw her away if she didn't 'get fixed,' she was willing to do whatever it took not to be cast out again. She wasn't going to take any more abandonment.

Carrie moved in and lived with me for a season. I began to understand how to access different parts of the soul realm. The scriptures opened up to me as I studied and tried to help her get free. The Lord highlighted all the places that talk about an undivided heart. David said, "Give me an undivided heart." Even the Psalmist's cry to God was that God would put him back together with an undivided heart.

> *Teach me your way, LORD, that I may rely on your*
> *faithfulness; give me an undivided heart, that I may*
> *fear your name (Psalm 86:11, NIV).*

It wasn't long after Carrie showed up in my life that I heard about a man named Dr. Joe Albright. A friend told me that this man knew how to put people back together, so I got his number and called him to see if he could teach me how to help the people God was sending to me. He only took appointment calls twice a year and his calendar was filled up six months ahead! When I finally reached him, he said his calendar was full and I should try again in six months. I asked if he could just answer a few questions for me. God was sending me people who were disassociated, medicated, suicidal, or divided in so many ways. "I need more tools, and I am praying you can help," I told him.

"Come for ministry. I don't release anyone to pray for the broken until I know that they are free themselves. Call me again in six months and see if you can get on my calendar," he said.

"Yes, sir," I said, obediently.

I'd never felt the level of authority I felt as this man spoke to me over the phone. I hung up. *Okay God, what now?* I couldn't wait six months! Carrie was living in my house and all these people were showing up all the time. I needed training now! Dr. Albright had been my hope.

23

Ten minutes later my phone rang. I heard that same strong voice on the other end of the phone. "Little lady, God must be on your side. I just got a cancellation and the Lord told me to give it to you."

I went to *learn*, and Dr. Albright became a lifeline for me. I spent the next season of my life learning from this wonderful man everything I could about the division of the soul and the powers of darkness. To this day, I have never met anyone who moved in the authority of God, who understood the power that Christ has delegated to His Church, the way Dr. Albright did.

I began to understand the principle of brokenness, and the existence of parts and pieces. How many times have you heard someone say, "I don't know, it's like a part of me is dead," or, "A part of me is so mad I want to kill him!" Or maybe you've even said yourself, "I'm so hurt. There's a part of me that still aches whenever I see that person." There are parts and there are pieces, and we have to access all of them, because that's where the healing is needed. We must take the power of the Cross to the precise location in the wounded soul. This, and more, I learned, and I thank God for my time in his shadow and all the things that he taught me.

Think of the stories you've heard of men in war zones or prison camps, and children who've survived terrible abuse or abandonment. Witness the terrible brokenness of children who have been kidnapped and used in the sex trade. Life has so much pain, but God, in His infinite wisdom, created us so marvelously that we can go through almost anything and survive. I minister to people every day who have survived it, and God wants to visit the broken places and bring the power of His precious blood to all of them.

Power to Heal

The day after that Junior High Bible study, the girls who had been in the room told all their friends what happened. As I was still seeking God for more of Himself, for keys to help people and see them free and whole, revival began to break out through the school. Students wanted to know more of Jesus, and they wanted to be free. The principal called me to figure out what I was all about, and ended up allowing the girls and I to use a classroom so that anyone who wanted prayer could be excused from class to come be prayed for. There was a steady stream of young people getting right with God, getting down on their knees, weeping and confessing their sins. Then they were going to church on Sundays and talking about the things God had done in their lives. There was definitely a buzz happening. We were all beginning to believe that God really means what He says in the Bible.

Submit yourselves, then, to God. Resist the devil, and he will flee from you. Come near to God and

*He will come near to you. Wash your hands, you
sinners, and purify your hearts, you double-minded
(James 4:7-10, NIV).*

Not everything was good, however. During this season, something awful happened. My niece, Sonia, was working at the church
as a custodian, trying to make ends meet. She often took her two
little boys, aged four and six, to work with her. One day they were
gathering trash and putting it in a dumpster outside the church by
the side of the road. Jim, her son, climbed to the top of the dumpster and Aaron, his brother, passed the bags up to him. Jim jumped
down just as a car came by, hit him and ran over him. The driver
screeched to a halt, rushed to carry him, unconscious, inside. They
called 911, and the ambulance came and took him to a trauma hospital in Austin. It was from the hospital that Sonia called me, undone
and begging me to come quickly and pray for him. When I got to
the hospital, Jim was in the ICU with a serious head trauma, and we
were told he might not make it through the night.

The Lord had me bind the spirit of death and speak life over
Jim. I believed God had the power to heal, but I was just learning
how to partner with that. The sweet little boy made it to the next day,
but his brain continued to swell. Sonia, his 21-year-old mother, was
alone and so scared she couldn't stay in the room for more than a few
minutes at a time. She begged me to stay with them. We had noticed
that the monitors went crazy every time I left the room, even just to
go to the bathroom, so I stayed. I kept praying over him, singing
over him, quoting scriptures and telling him that he was going to be
okay. They said his brain would continue to swell for days, and that
the pressure against his skull might kill him. They told us his mind
wasn't there, but I knew it was; I could feel it. I kept talking to him
and telling him that Jesus would heal him and he would be okay. The
presence of God was in the room, and we were fighting for his life.

On the third day a respiratory therapist came to give him a breathing treatment. She didn't know he had been unconscious for three days. When she put the device close to his mouth he woke up and pushed it away. She tried again.

"Leave him alone. He's awake!" I told her.

He opened his eyes, looked at me and said, "Why do I have a diaper on? Take it off me!"

I told him we'd get it off soon and that he should lie still until the doctor came. He was ready to climb out of that bed! He was sitting up, wide awake and full of questions. We were all so excited! His doctor came in and examined him, telling us they would move him out of ICU and into a regular room. We moved our things to the other room, but before they could even put him into bed another doctor came and told us there was nothing more to do. They were releasing him, instead! We went home that very day. God had given Jim back to us.

Through this experience I learned that you can't look at what *seems* to be happening in the physical realm. You must look to God. Even with no signs of life or any chance of recovery, we kept looking to God for His power. God gave us a choice that day, and we chose life!

> *This day I call the heavens and the earth as witnesses against you that I have set before you life and death, blessings, and curses. Now choose life, so that you and yours may live (Deuteronomy 30:19, NIV).*

God was still moving at the school where my children attended. They made lots of new friends, and our home became a place where kids would come and hang out. I was in the kitchen one day when I heard the children calling me. They'd been jumping on the trampoline and when I went to check on them, they were helping their friend, Tommy, to sit down on the deck. "I think it's broken," one of them said. I saw that the bone in his leg was pressing outwards, pushing the skin up. Yep, definitely broken. I asked him if he knew where his mother was and told him we needed to call her and get him to the Emergency Room.

"Can't God heal this?" he questioned, looking up at me. He'd been hearing stories of all the powerful things God was doing. And he *believed*.

"Yes, He can," I said.

I thought we would pray and then go to the Emergency Room. I put my hand over the break and the children and I prayed, "God, you can do this. Show us Your power to heal!"

Tommy then stretched his leg straight out, completely healed with only a bruise to show what had happened. The kids never even came into the house. They went right back to playing.

On another occasion, my son Joel was playing soccer at school when he broke his ankle. The team and the coach prayed for him as soon as it happened. He came home on crutches with his ankle purple, black, and blue, and swollen to twice the normal size. As I drove him to the doctor, I wrestled with God. "I know You can heal him! This is his senior year and his basketball team is going to State. You're his Father, and I need You to take care of this!"

I was a desperate woman petitioning for my son, and I let God hear my cry for sure that day.

The doctor said it looked like a break, but he would take an X-Ray to make sure. "You've injured it in the same place you broke it last time," he said, looking at the X-Ray.

"But he's never broken it before," I said, "Would we have known if he had?

He laughed. "Would you have known if he'd broken it? Oh, yes."

Joel *had* broken his ankle the day before, but God had healed the break overnight! The bones were restored and you could see it on the x-ray. The muscles and tendons were the only strain that remained, and they healed very quickly. He was able to continue to play basketball and go to State Playoffs with his team that year!

These are just a few examples of how we learned to be a family that expected the supernatural, and to call on God for His power to heal. He has been so faithful. We would pray first, then go to doctors . . . if He directed us to. He didn't always, and I learned early on that God not only had the power to heal, but *wanted* to heal His people.

———✺———

One day my friend Kay and I were in my kitchen when there was a knock at the door. Five Hispanic ladies from the Austin area were on my porch. Only one or two of them spoke broken English.

"Who sent you?" I asked.

"A lady told us if we'd come to you, you'd pray."

One of the ladies had an eye infection. Her doctors were afraid to operate because the infection could possibly spread to her brain. The eye was swelling, and her friends were afraid it would burst. Doctors couldn't do anything for her; only God could heal her, so they had come. The woman was sitting on the couch, and we sat there for several moments, looking at each other. I didn't know what to pray, but as I closed my eyes, I remembered that Jesus had taken his spit, made it into mud and put it on someone's eye.

And some people brought to Jesus a blind man and
begged him to touch him. And he took the blind man
by the hand, led him out of the village, and when he

had spit on his eyes and laid his hands on him, Jesus asked, "Do you see anything?" He looked up and said, "I see people, but they look like trees walking." Then Jesus laid his hands on his eyes again; and he opened his eyes, his sight was restored, and he saw everything clearly (Mark 8:22-25, ESV).

He wants me to spit on her eye! I rubbed my finger across my lips to get it a little bit damp, went over and touched her eye. I knew that if I was obedient to the Lord, I would see His power.

"God, You can do this," I prayed. "You see her heart and her faith. You know the need. Heal her Jesus, give her back her sight." I backed up and said, "Open your eyes, what do you see?"

She looked at me. "I can see you."

"Close the good eye and tell me what you see with the other one."

"It looks kind of like trees."

When she said that, immediately my faith grew. I thought of the Bible story! "Okay! Close your eyes again." Again, I rubbed my fingers against my lips. I went over and touched her eye and said, "Finish what You're doing here, God. Show us Your glory. Show us Your power. Restore what the locusts have stolen."

"Now what do you see?" I asked.

"I can see you!"

"Close your good eye."

"I can see you! I can see you!" she exclaimed with excitement.

I felt the Lord put His own DNA into her body. We carry the blood of Christ in our bodies, so we have His DNA. Since that day, the Lord has prompted me to gently apply DNA when He's going to create new body parts for healing. Creative miracles like a new eyeball require the DNA of our Creator. The power of Jesus is in the blood of Jesus. The shedding of His blood has empowered the

Church to do everything He did, and even greater works! God wants us, the Church, to know we are joint heirs with Christ. We carry His DNA, and He is the creator and the healer of ALL things.

I looked at her one last time and said, "Have you always had one green eye and one brown eye?"

"What do you mean? I have brown eyes!"

"Well, one is green, and one is brown," I said, and her friend looked at her and agreed. The woman jumped up and ran into the bathroom to look in the mirror.

"I have a new eye! God has given me a new eye!"

It was a sign and a wonder. Her eye didn't just get healed, He actually gave her a brand-new eye! He did things in her that day and used them as a sign to all who were there with her. He does a new thing. He does what He wants to do, how He wants to, and when He wants to. It was powerful and wonderful.

> *See, I am doing a new thing! Now it springs up; do you not perceive it? I am making a way in the wilderness and streams in the wasteland (Isaiah 43:19, NIV).*

Healings were one of the first signs God used to draw people to me to get healed and whole. I read the Bible and believed what it said. My kids, friends and I started believing God, and praying for people to be healed. If you never pray for healing, you will never see it. But if you start asking – if you take the Bible at its word – you just might begin to see amazing things!

Power to be Made Whole

God wasn't just healing kids, and He wasn't just healing physical problems. I was asking Him to do lots of things: teach me, train me, heal people, deliver people, provide my needs, bring freedom… I asked him for everything, and He was doing it all! I was learning as much as I could, as fast as I could, even though I didn't understand a lot of the things that were happening. I had a circle of dear friends who were hungry for Jesus. Just like me, they didn't understand all that God was teaching us, or all that He was up to, but they were right there with me.

> *I tell you the truth, anyone who believes in me will do the same works I have done, and even greater works, because I am going to be with the Father. You can ask for anything in my name, and I will do it, so that the Son can bring glory to the Father (John 14:12;13, NLT).*

Norma was a dear friend who offered her home to help with many things as the ministry unfolded. Over the years, we met at Norma's countless times for Bible study, prayer, and worship. Though she is in her eighties now, she is still a faithful friend, loyal supporter, and fierce prayer warrior. One day at Norma's, I walked in and saw a woman sitting on the sofa.

"Hi. My name is Viva. A friend told me that I should come here, and that you would pray for me and I would be healed."

Viva told me she had not slept in months. I touched her and out she went, dropping to the sofa, sound asleep under the power of God. I never even prayed for her. We carried on with Bible Study, worshipping loudly as she slept peacefully on Norma's couch. When we wrapped up an hour and a half later, she woke up. I asked if she wanted prayer. She said no, adding that she felt fine and didn't even need prayer! We said goodbye and she left, knowing that God had touched her.

The next day I got a call from a man.

"You prayed for my wife last night and I need to come see you." I couldn't tell from his tone of voice if this was going to be a pleasant meeting or not. I had already begun to experience that when the power of God is poured out, some people do not like it. Even Christians. For some reason, we often get offended by things we don't understand. I was already beginning to experience people misunderstanding me, judging me, distancing themselves from me, and even accusing me. I could not tell if this man was happy about what God was doing in his wife, or upset and blaming me. I made an appointment to see him a couple of days later.

"My wife came home from your Bible Study and slept through the whole night. I woke up in the night to find her sleeping soundly. She hasn't slept through the night since I've known her. And I wanted to tell you this: When I woke up in the night, I smelled something familiar that I haven't smelled since I was a teenager. It was the fragrance of Christ."

He went on to say that as a young man he felt called to the ministry. At the same time, he felt a strong pull to join the military. His pastor had told him he had to choose one or the other. Thinking he wouldn't be able to do both, he signed up for the military, where he had had a brilliant career as a Green Beret. But over the years he had walked away from his relationship with God, believing he let God down by not becoming a pastor. We were able to pray through that and he and his wife began to come regularly to our home. He got back into a right relationship with God and she met Jesus and got free from the torment that came to her in the night. The Kingdom of God came into their family. Everyone got saved, healed, and delivered. The fragrance of Christ filled their entire lives!

> *His young shoots will grow. His splendor will be like an olive tree, His fragrance like a cedar of Lebanon (Hosea 14:6, NIV).*

> *Your lips drop sweetness as the honeycomb, my bride; milk and honey are under your tongue. The fragrance of your garments is like the fragrance of Lebanon (Song of Songs 4:11, NIV).*

Another man came to me who was suffering terribly. The Harvard School of Medicine had told him he had the worst PTSD they had ever seen! Research has shown that PTSD opens the door to many diseases and greatly shortens life expectancy. He had been diagnosed with several life-threatening diseases. Diabetes, high blood pressure, heart disease and depression were just some of his medical problems.

I asked the Lord to bring me the part of him that had been traumatized. He told me terrible things he had seen and lived through, including witnessing a lot of death. I had him open the door to Jesus, and as Jesus walked through his memories with him, the landscape of his mind began to change. After we had prayed through all the memories his countenance began to change, too. The depression and hopelessness were gone, replaced with the peace of Christ.

He was so changed that night that when he got home his wife accused him of drinking too much and made him sleep on the couch! He was completely healed and set free. Within a few weeks he had a completely different diagnosis. No more high blood pressure, and the diabetes had disappeared. His doctors were amazed, and so were we. God proved Himself mighty again!

I was beginning to see that, not only did God want to heal our bodies, but he wanted our souls to be made whole, as well. And many times, the healing of our bodies follows the healing of our souls. God wants to heal it all.

> *He restoreth my soul: He leadeth me in the paths*
> *of righteousness for His name's sake (Psalm 23:3,*
> *KJV).*

One Sunday, I was asked to be on the altar team at the front of the church. At the end of the service, there was an altar call. A college girl came to me for prayer. When I laid my hands on her, she began to weep; I could sense she was coming back to the Lord. Her life turned around that day. I spent several years discipling her, loving on her and watching her grow in the Lord. At one point her mother called me from the Dallas area. Her daughter was home from school and she had seen the change in her life. I was a bit nervous. I have been accused on more than one occasion of brainwashing the college kids I was discipling. I suppose, in fact, that was my destiny, to wash their brains clean! I wanted to wash away the pain and trauma, and all the false beliefs they had been taught. I wanted them to be cleansed of everything that kept them from Jesus.

The girl's mother was named Barbara, and it turned out that she'd been praying for me ever since she'd seen the change in her daughter. She, herself, had just been diagnosed with cancer and had a large tumor on her breast. She told me the Lord told her that if I would pray the tumor would disappear. I was glad the Lord had told her that, but He certainly hadn't told me!

So here she came to church one day, a woman with a huge tumor, and a surgeon who said she needed it removed at once. I prayed for her, laid my hand right on the tumor on her breast – which was hard for me to do right in the middle of the sanctuary at church – and said, "God if you're going to heal her, heal her." She went home after the service and found the tumor was gone. I was probably more surprised than anyone! She and I became great friends and saw each other often through the years.

A few years later, I got another call from Barbara. This time it was her husband, John, who had cancer. He had kidney cancer and was given only three months to live. John had recently retired from a major oil company. He had traveled extensively, making contracts with companies in the Middle East. It was a high-profile job and he was a successful man whose life had been focused on working and providing. As soon as he retired, they found out he had cancer.

Barbara's husband had never walked with God. He'd never been to church with her. He wasn't interested in her religion or her God. I asked her if he would like to see me for prayer, and she said yes, but I was pretty sure he was only coming because she wanted him to. Regardless, they made the trip. It was a long drive for a very sick man.

When they arrived, I introduced my friends Michelle and Kay, whom I had invited to join us. As we all began to pray for John, I felt the heavens shift. The atmosphere began to change and I started to weep as I looked at John. As I waited for God to give me the words to pray, I felt God's heart toward this man. I looked straight into his eyes and said, "God is more concerned about your soul than your body. What have you done with God? What have you done with His Son Jesus, the one who died for you?"

He looked at me and said, "I've been busy with work and with my family and I've never done anything with God. What do I need to do?"

I told him he needed to commit his life to Jesus. That he needed to pray and ask God to forgive him for his sins and let Him come into his life. He asked me if there was anything specific that he should say to God. "Say that you want to get to know Him and you're thankful for His love and the way He's taken care of you and your family."

He nodded his head and he prayed, "Jesus I want to get to know you, and I want You to come and be a part of my life and my family. I'm so thankful for the way You've taken care of us through the years. Please come and forgive me and change me and heal me. In Jesus' name, Amen."

While we were praying, I noticed Michelle had left the house. She came back in the front door a moment later. After the couple left, I asked her what she was doing outside.

"I have never felt what I felt when you began to pray," she said. "I knew I was standing in an open heaven, so I went outside to see if there was a manifestation in the sky, and there was! A circle of light was coming down over the house. There were clouds all around, but an open heaven over the house. I just wanted to see it."

I was so surprised. I had no idea that Heaven would respond in a natural way, but we all knew that God had stepped into that room.

And this man, who all his life made contracts with important businesses, had now made the most important contract with the King of Heaven, and he would be there for all eternity.

John didn't die in a few months. He lived a few more years. The testimony of his wife and daughters was that he was a changed man. He was kind. He was loving and gentle. It was a whole different side of the father and husband than they had known. They were so thankful God had given him a few more years, and that he'd committed his life to God. And most of all they were thankful for the day that the heavens opened up over a little house in the country and John signed a contract with the Living God.

> *May God himself, the God who makes everything holy and whole, make you holy and whole, put you together – spirit, soul, and body – and keep you fit for the coming of our Master, Jesus Christ. The one who called you is completely dependable. If he said it, he will do it (1 Thessalonians, 5:23-24, MSG)*

The Core

I was teaching kindergarten, raising four children, hanging on and fighting for my marriage and my family, teaching Bible Study, and ministering to anyone who showed up broken. I knew of many deliverance and inner healing ministries, and I knew many people who came to me had tried many of these things. An addict, for example, would come to me and say they'd had inner healing and 'it worked for a while,' but then something would happen and they'd go right back to their old ways. I didn't understand this, and I wanted God to show me how to be more effective. I had so much going on, I didn't have time to waste! I also believed that God came to destroy the works of the evil one and give us abundant life. I wanted to see this abundance!

Then one day I saw a scripture in a new way.

> *Behold, you desire truth in the inward parts (Psalm 51:6, NKJV).*

God had already taught me about fractures. People would come to me and tell me about their broken parts – some hurt or trauma to their soul – something horrible that had happened. We would pray, forgive, and get those *parts* healed and whole. But they had other parts. When I saw this scripture that day, God spoke to me. There weren't just fractures and broken parts in us. There is an innermost part, like a control center, or the root of life, and God wants to take healing all the way to the depths of us.

I began to call this The Core. It is one of the foundational principles of Beth Shalom that is different than any other inner healing or deliverance ministry I have ever been a part of or learned from. When someone comes to me and tells me something they struggle with, or something that happened to them, we could go in and handle that one part, but the Bible speaks many times about patterns.

> *Do not conform to the patterns of this world, but be transformed by the renewing of your mind (Romans 12:2, NIV).*

What I began to learn is that if I could get to the core of someone's soul and bring God's light and healing there, all the other broken fractures in them would be healed and become whole as well. They come into alignment with who they are at their very core. The patterns of sin or the patterns of lies that were planted in the core of them stop repeating.

There was a woman who had come to me several times for ministry and healing. I had worked with her and walked with her, and God had healed so many things in her life and put her back together in so many ways. She'd struggled with mental torment, and God had healed her of that. She'd had so many broken relationships, yet there had been much reconciliation and she now had a tight-knit group of good friends. She had a good job and was pursuing the things of

God. We had gotten a lot of fractures forgiven and healed, but she still had major issues in one area… her relationship with her mother.

She knew she had to forgive. Every time something would come up, she would forgive it and try to move past it with her mom, but there was always tension. Forgiveness and peace only seemed to last so long when it came to her mom. But when God started showing me about The Core, I thought, "That's it. Something is so deep that it goes all the way to her core. That's why she can't forgive it or move past it."

I explained to her what God was revealing to me about The Core –that he had shown me a place deep in our souls. I showed her Psalms 51:6 that talks about 'the inmost parts,' where God desires truth and wisdom. I told her what we had done over the years was to go to the places in her soul that were damaged from trauma and lies, and that had helped so much. But, I explained, I now believed there was a core, and that some traumas could have been there from the very beginning, gone so deep, or affected her so much, that the center of who she was had been damaged. And our tie to our mother in the womb is surely at the very beginning and, if the enemy had any access, could be used to damage our core.

So we prayed and asked the Lord to go to the deep places. We asked God to bring up any memories or trauma that might be all the way down to her core. And we waited. And waited. We asked the Lord to show her a memory, a picture, a feeling, a phrase. She began to cry.

"What do you see, or hear, or feel?" I asked. God uses all of our senses to speak to us. She felt first.

"I'm cold, and I'm wet," she said. "I'm so cold." And then she began to see.

"There are wooden bars. I'm behind them."

"Like a jail cell?" I asked.

"I'm really little and there are empty bottles around me. I know my mom is outside my door but she won't come in. Why won't she come in?"

As the memories unfolded, we found a neglected, abandoned baby, alone in her crib, crying for a mother who would not come. For whatever reason, the mother would leave her untended in the crib. The memories of longing for her mother, of crying out for her help and not being responded to, was lodged so deeply at the root of her, that as an adult, she could not trust her mother. She felt so abandoned, neglected and rejected – right down to her Core – that forgiving the circumstances she experienced as an adult was not working.

I had learned that Jesus would heal anything we ask Him to, but often times people only ask to heal a certain memory, or a certain hurt. This woman had Jesus walk her through the trauma of specific memories, specific hurts. And her life was different. But she needed to be healed all the way to her Core. The baby who was taught that she could not rely on her mother needed to be healed, and the lie that she had no one to take care of her needed to be broken off of who she was.

A shift took place in her relationship with her mom from that day on. She could finally let go of things her mom did. She wasn't so angry or so triggered. She could actually enjoy her relationship.

———————

I will talk about The Core more in later chapters on lies and generational iniquity. It shifted how efficient and effective I was in ministry. It began to make God's work much faster and much more effective. In fact, learning about this helped heal some recurring patterns in my own life. I had always struggled with feelings that I didn't belong. I felt it with my brothers growing up, I'd felt it at church, I'd felt it partying with friends in high school, and I'd felt it in my marriage. Now, God was doing all of these amazing things in and through me, but I still had these little inner thoughts like, "This is not for you," or "You don't really belong here." They didn't make any sense.

My parents were planners. They wanted two children. My mother planned to go back to teaching when her second child entered kindergarten. They had two boys, ages four and six, when my mother found out she was pregnant with me. I was not in the plan. They had struggled on one income for six years so she could stay home with my brothers. When she realized I was on the way, their plans were pushed back another five years.

I was being prayed for one day when I had a memory from the womb of this. The man leading me in prayer said, "God, take her to the place in her soul where this feeling first started." Immediately, I knew I was having a memory from the womb. I know that sounds strange, but God had been sending me people who'd had these things happen, and I knew He was trying to teach me something.

I could feel, and hear, my mother's heartbeat. I could feel her anxiety and panic, and I could hear my parent's yelling. My daddy yelled, "What were you thinking? We don't even have a place for another child."

As a very tiny new life, I felt everything my mom felt, and I heard everything my dad said. From that time on I felt like I had no place and no plan. For thirty years I believed my life was a mistake and there was no room in my family for me. It made no sense. My parents loved me and took care of me when I was born, but even before I had been born, I believed a lie that had been planted at the core of who I was because of something I heard and felt inside the womb.

When God revealed that memory to me, a cloud lifted off my soul. I had handled so many fractures and forgiven so many broken parts of my life, and they had all had the same pattern or theme: I didn't think I belonged. I behaved, or allowed someone to treat me as if there was no space for me, over and over again in different areas of my life. But handling this core memory, I could finally believe that I was wanted and loved. Bringing the truth to my core and healing it there rippled to all the other areas of my life that had been affected by my core.

Everything started to come together in my mind. I began to understand that God's plan was for me to help people find freedom in Christ. Every day had purpose, and I knew I had a destiny.

I had asked the Lord for 'power tools' as I worked with people. I was doing more and more all the time. More and more broken people were showing up at my house. I was teaching. I was raising my children. I needed God to make me more efficient and effective, or I needed it all to stop. The Core was a major power tool. I could find the pattern of lies or trauma and replace them with the truth, or with healing, and it would ripple out to all of the other broken pieces and fractures of their soul.

It was so awesome! And the best part was, it destroyed the works of the enemy.

The Unfolding of Destiny

The things I was experiencing were strange. God was teaching me about forgiveness and fractures, the core of who we are, and the demonic. I'd grown up in church and never heard these things taught, yet I was seeing the truth of them every day as people asked me to pray for them. I was starting to see the power of God more and more, but it was also starting to cost me more and more. People were talking about me, and not aways positively. It was taking more of my time and becoming more inconvenient. I really didn't know what I was doing and I didn't understand what was happening.

But God needed me to understand, so He gave me a series of encounters that let me know without a shadow of a doubt that what was happening to me and through me was Him, it was on purpose. He also revealed that it was for a much bigger calling than I could have imagined.

One Wednesday night, my family went to eat dinner at church before the Wednesday night service. I was trying to get to my young kids to eat when two women walked past me.   One of the women came back, leaned over the table, and stuck her finger in my face,

"Who are you?"

"My name is Monte."

"No, not your name," she said. "Who are you?"

"I'm the children's pastor, I work with the kids."

"No. That's not it. Who are you?" she asked again.

"I'm a wife and a mother."

She repeated, "No. WHO are you?"

I thought for a minute. *Lord, who am I?* I realized what she was talking about. "Deliverance?"

"Yes!" she said. "That's what it is!"

She leaned in closer and said, "The Lord told me to tell you that what is in you is not from you; it is from Heaven. God put it there and it's for His purpose. You will do what you were created to do. It is from God, and you need to know it's from God." Then she looked at me and said, almost apologetically, "I don't know why I said all that, I just know God told me to." And she walked away.

What she didn't know was that just that morning I had told God I didn't understand the things that were going on inside of me. I didn't know why more and more traumatized, broken people were hearing about me, calling me, and showing up at my house. I was seeing incredible healings and breakthrough, but it was also beginning to affect my children, my reputation, and every area of my life.

I didn't understand why some people at church were angry with me because of what I was doing to help people find freedom. I didn't understand all the persecution and confusion. Out of all the people on this planet, it should have been believers who understood me the most. People at church didn't know what to do with me, though, because they were seeing and hearing of things happening that they'd never seen or heard of before, even though they'd been in church their whole lives.

I had told God that very morning that if He didn't show up and tell me what was going on, I would walk away from all of it. After this encounter with a stranger, I knew that He had heard me, so I began to dig deeper into whatever this was that He was calling me to.

That was the day Michelle Hollon came into my life and became my mentor. Our relationship began when she spoke that word over me. You see, Michelle had been involved in deliverance for years, and she understood all that I was walking through. She'd experienced the ups and downs and had encounters with God and with demons. She understood the opposition I was facing from the demonic and from church, and began to pray for me. I had prayed God would send me someone who understood, someone who could teach me.

Many people began coming to me who were demonized. People who had multiple and split personalities, schizophrenia, diseases, patterns of sin they had tried everything to break... desperate, tormented people who didn't know where to go or what to do. God sent them to me and I could see past the demons into their hearts. I could feel the love God had for them. I was angry at what the demons had done to their lives and I commanded those demons to go. I wasn't always sure what I was doing, but it seemed to work, and more and more people kept coming.

> *God is faithful, who has called you into fellowship*
> *with His Son, Jesus Christ our Lord (1 Corinthians*
> *1:9, NIV).*

When God is doing something in your life, there are often periods of confusion, emptiness , periods where it feels as if He has left. That "aloneness" can feel relentless. There were years of challenge in my daily life as God was sharpening my senses to hear Him, see Him, feel Him, and even taste and smell His presence. Life was still happening. I had little kids. I had a husband who had walked away from the Lord and was battling his own demons, which meant I had my own heartbreak and struggles as well. And every single day I had to choose if I believed God, if I wanted more of what He was doing and showing me, if I was going to be obedient when things looked weird or hard, or seemed silent. And every day I chose Him. Every day I told the Lord He could do with me whatever he wanted. Every day I prayed to be a carrier of His presence. I studied the "Ark of the Covenant." I wanted to be a place where His glory would rest.

There were years of fasting during which I heard, *I want you to fast for twenty-one days,* or *forty days,* or *for three days,* or *to take no solid food.* I did one fast and then another. Once the Lord told me to wear only Camo clothing! This made no sense to me until I realized this was a fast from worrying about how I looked and what I wore. God wanted me free from vanity and anxiety. I learned not to be concerned about what anyone around me thought of me!

> *Therefore, I tell you, do not worry about your life,*
> *what you will eat or drink; or about your body,*
> *what you will wear. Is not life more than food, and*
> *the body more than clothes (Matthew 6:25, NIV)?*

Then God told me to fast from using first person pronouns. There were so many outside attacks on my reputation that I had slipped into trying to defend myself. God reminded me that He is my Defender, and that I didn't have to be concerned for my own well-being . . . that was His job. So I disciplined myself to turn my attention away from me. I went for a season without using the words "I," "me," or "mine." When I caught myself using one of these words, I corrected it. Over time I became less preoccupied with myself and more concerned about the needs of others. When I had a thought that was arrogant or self-seeking, I repented of it and confessed it to Kay, my best friend and a spiritual warrior who walked beside me. God wanted me spiritually strong, but not to feel spiritually superior! By confessing these thoughts to my friend and then praying, God set me free from these attitudes. He wanted to change me and restore me. He was going deep within me and changing the motives behind the way I thought.

All a person's ways seem pure to them, but motives are weighed by the Lord (Proverbs 16:2, NIV).

Mixed motives twist life into tangles. Pure motives take you straight down the road (Proverbs 21:8, MSG).

In Exodus Chapter 25, I learned that the inside of the Ark of the Covenant was made of pure gold. If I wanted to carry God's presence with supernatural signs and wonders, I would need to be polished and pure on the inside. If my inmost parts, my motives and my desires were "pure gold," I would be able to carry His presence and do what Jesus did, just as He promised we would do.

This season of fasts went on for years. One day, my friend Penny came to me and said, "I have a word for you that I believe is from God. It doesn't make sense to me, but I believe He wants me to tell you this. He says you don't need to fast anymore. Your whole life has become a fast to Him."

I understood immediately. I didn't need to worry about what fast He would call me to do next; my life itself had been set apart for Him. I would learn to do only what I saw the Father do. The Lord directed me to this Scripture:

> *"Is not this the kind of fasting I have chosen: to loose*
> *the chains of injustice and untie the cords of the*
> *yoke, to set the oppressed free and break every yoke?*
> *Is it not to share your food with the hungry and*
> *to provide the poor wanderer with shelter—when*
> *you see the naked, to clothe them, and not to turn*
> *away from your own flesh and blood (Isaiah 58:6;7,*
> *NIV)?*

God taught me to hear Him and respond quickly to what He commanded. It often came with great challenges to me, personally. But it was also a season of incredible joy! I saw more and more of His Power working as I simply obeyed His voice.

Just weeks before my mother's death, she stood by my kitchen counter and waited for me to stop and look up from what I was doing.

"The Lord spoke to me this morning," she said. "He told me that you are the one He promised to your father and me. Years ago, I was praying about whether to marry your dad, and the Lord told me that he was the one for me. When I asked him why, He said He was going to give us a child who would be in full-time ministry. Your father and I always thought that child would be Paul [my oldest brother], and we were crushed by his early death. Now I know that it was you God promised us would serve Him full-time."

"But I'm just a wife and a mother. I don't have a ministry."

"I've lived with you now for almost seven years. A steady stream of people have come to this house, and all of them have received Jesus in some way. I know I have given the Lord the child He asked me to carry and raise."

As my mom saw me moving in my destiny, she came to know that she had, in part, fulfilled her own destiny. It was a divine, healing moment for both of us.

———

One Sunday morning I was on the stage, worshipping with my eyes closed. When I opened them, I saw a very tall man with long, black arms raised high as he worshipped, completely absorbed. There was something very different about him, and I was drawn to him. I closed my eyes again and the thought came to me that he might be an angel. When I opened my eyes again, he was gone. But I saw him later in the sanctuary kneeling down with his face to the ground, lost in praise and worship.

After the service, I left through the center door and there was the same tall man. When he saw me, he knelt down in front of me, raised his long arms up and began to prophesy.

"You are highly-favored of God. You are known in all of Heaven." My church was NOT a place where this sort of thing happened, and I was embarrassed. He continued talking, but I turned and went to my car with my friend Pam. I was uncomfortable with the things he was saying. He didn't even know me, and I didn't know what to think. I just knew I didn't want to draw any more attention, so Pam and I left.

Later that afternoon, Pam and I were sitting on my back porch when the tall, dark stranger came around the corner of my deck. I was totally surprised to see him at my house, and he looked just as surprised to see me. My home is fifteen miles from town and can be hard to find.

"What are you doing here? How did you know where I live?"

"I didn't know," he said.

"Well, what's your name?

"Aaron."

I knew that Aaron means "the mouthpiece of God." He began to prophesy again, speaking about the ministry and the property, rather than about me. At this time, I didn't have a real ministry. Sure, I had spent time with people who came to the house, listening and praying through their difficulties. But I was working as a kindergarten teacher, and only prayed for people when I got home from work.

"You will minister to hundreds and to thousands," he continued. "Your ministry will be international and bring many to freedom. There is a double anointing on you and this ministry."

Just as he spoke the words "double anointing," two huge white doves swooped down onto the deck, and just as quickly flew away. These were not Texas doves, which are smaller and more brown in color. They were twice the size of any dove Pam or I had ever seen. Big, beautiful white birds that appeared and disappeared right before our eyes.

"The winds have changed," Aaron said. And just as he said it, the wind changed direction and started to pick up. Pam's and my hair blew and we felt the coolness of a breeze that came out of nowhere, like the wind that comes before a cold front. It was like a scene from a movie, but it was real, and it was happening in front of me!

"I see legions of angels coming to stand by you and strengthen you. Legions and legions of angels are coming. They will protect you and the ministry. You will never be afraid again," he said, waving his outstretched arms above his head.

There was wheat in the field that year, and as the wind blew, it seemed as if the wheat was bowing down. Once more, I couldn't help but think that it felt like a movie . . . or a dream. Pam and I were caught up in the sights and sounds of another dimension. Aaron vanished from the deck and came back later with a white dishtowel over his wrist, like a waiter. He produced a platter of cheeses and grapes, and a glass of wine. He said to relax and enjoy. Dinner would be served in forty-five minutes! Pam laughed and laughed. I was so glad she was there, because I wouldn't have believed it had really happened.

"I love coming to see you," she said. "Every time I come we see the supernatural. The Lord brought me here to witness what He is doing in your ministry."

Forty-five minutes later, Aaron reappeared and said, "Dinner is served." Inside, the table was set and the meal was delicious. Two of my sons were there and joined us. Typically, they had plenty to say, but were uncharacteristically quiet.

As Aaron continued to affirm me in the eyes of God, he turned to my sons. "Do you have any idea who your mother is?"

"We do," said the boys. I seemed to be the only one who didn't know who I was!

Aaron got me to tell stories of the things I had seen God do in our house. Stories of broken bones being knit together; deaf ears opened; a new eye appearing in place of a blind one. Stories of addictions being broken, visions of angels, people being healed of diseases; people who showed up on my doorstep, wanting to die, but who left free and eager to step into their destiny. He seemed to know how to draw the stories out of me, and it was amazing to put it all together and hear myself say it out loud. God had done great things, and testifying out loud made me know deep in myself that it had all been on purpose.

I had seen so many powerful things happen, and had heard God speaking and teaching. After that stranger stopped me at church and told me my destiny, after my mother spoke to me about my destiny... after Aaron the angel served me lunch and told me who I was... I gave up! I completely surrendered my will to the call of God on my life.

Everything changed after that day. Fear left my life and no longer kept me from doing things. People began to see angels in and around my house. Within a year, my house and my other debts were paid off. I quit my job and began full time ministry. The windows of Heaven seemed to open and people and provision flowed in and out. Beth Shalom was granted Non-Profit status and I began to travel and minister both nationwide and internationally. That summer, I flew to Mexico to minister. And then came a mission trip to Asia. Less than twelve months from my visitation from the tall, dark stranger, I had been to the other side of the world to bring wholeness to the broken. God is amazing!

I had friends – like my friends Kay and Pam from these stories – who were constant companions. They greatly encouraged me to embrace my destiny. God has plans for each one of us even before we are born. Stepping into our God-identities and moving in His purposes is the most fulfilling and joyous thing we can do in this life. No matter how long it takes, find people who will speak destiny over you. Find those who will remind you who you are and what God has said about you. Find your destiny and walk in it!

We are God's handiwork, created in Christ Jesus to do good works which God prepared in advance for us to do (Ephesians 2:10, NIV).

The Keys to the Kingdom

One night as I was getting ready for bed, I received a phone call. The woman on the other end of the phone said she was coming to see me the next day, and she let me know that I was her last resort. She didn't want to upset me, she said, but if she wasn't healed and set free, she was going to take her own life! She had been to faith healers, deliverance ministers, psychiatrists, counselors, medical doctors, and mental hospitals. She'd been counseled and medicated in every way possible, and none of it had helped.

"I don't want you to blame yourself if it doesn't work, because no one has been able to help me my entire life," she said.

"Come to my house tomorrow. I can't do anything for you but if you come, Jesus will meet with us, and He will heal you."

I hung up the phone and heard the enemy say, "Who do you think you are? What do you think you can do that everyone else couldn't do for her?" Panic and fear were suddenly at my door.

I cried out, "Jesus, what should I do?"

I have the keys, He said in a quiet, gentle tone.

I remembered what I had read in His Word about the keys to the kingdom belonging to His disciples. A peace swept over me that could only come from Jesus. I forgot the panic and began to feel good about what I would see God do the next day. I slept soundly the whole night through.

> *And I tell you, you are Peter, and on this rock, I will build my church, and the gates of hell shall not prevail against it. I will give you the keys of the kingdom of heaven, and whatever you bind on earth shall be bound in heaven, and whatever you loose on earth shall be loosed in heaven" (Matthew 16:18-19, ESV).*

The next morning, this precious woman was at my door. She quickly reminded me of our conversation on the phone the night before. "No worries," I said. "Jesus told me that He has the keys." We sat at the kitchen table and prayed, and she told me one of the most tragic stories I had ever heard.

She was one of the youngest children in a very large, very poor family. She was born with a birth defect, a cleft palate, and she was severely neglected and abused by both her parents. Her dad would get drunk and abuse her sexually and physically from the age of three. Her mom would withhold food, clothing and even affection. Her siblings were also cruel to her. They would take her food, shut her out of play, say cruel things to her, and even hit her.

The abuse was so severe that parts of her had literally died, causing severe issues in her life. In her ministry session, we located fractured inner children who were actually dead. The first was a three-year-old who had frozen to death outside her bedroom window after going outside to hide from her abusers. When we found the fracture, we both saw the same picture in our mind's eye.

She said, "Oh no, she's dead."

In my mind I saw a cold, blue baby girl huddled behind a bush, next to a house under a window. As I explained to her what I was seeing, she told me she used to crawl out of the window to escape the abuse.

"It's okay," I assured her. "I know Someone Who can raise the dead."

> *I am the Resurrection and the Life (John 11:25, KJV).*

At that moment in the vision, Jesus appeared, knelt down beside her and warmed her with His robes. As He breathed on her, the color came back into her face, and His life was breathed into the dead parts of her soul. He lifted her up and carried her back into the room, alive and well. We both wept! This was the first time I had seen the dead raised!

> *Yes, God raised Jesus to life! And since God's Spirit of Resurrection lives in you, He will also raise your dying body to life by the same Spirit that breathes life into you (Romans 8:11, TPT)!*

As I finished praying and opened my eyes, the woman in front of me looked completely different. Her face was shining! "I have always felt like a part of me was dead. Now I know why."

My eyes were opened to new levels of glory that day as I saw the resurrection power of Jesus quicken her body. I had a new tool, and I understood even more profoundly what Jesus was saying to His disciples:

Heal the sick, raise the dead, cleanse those who have leprosy, drive out demons. Freely you have received; freely give (Matthew 10:8, NIV).

I worked with this woman for several months and saw Jesus put her back together in an amazing way. She went on to work with broken girls in a residential home, and later with PTSD patients in the military. She also wrote a book on God's power to restore lives.

Another significant key was given to me when a woman showed up at my door and told me this story:

"I was bred in a Satanic cult to become the bride of Satan. My father and mother were brother and sister and I am what they call a 'blueblood.' I have six birth certificates with different names for me, but I don't think any of them are authentic."

For the next few hours, I heard some of the most gruesome stories I have ever heard about things no one should ever have to experience. She shared with me that she had been used in satanic rituals throughout her childhood. Her grandfather had raped her at the age of two to transfer his demons to her before he died. After years of neglect and abuse, she was able to escape at seventeen. She met Jesus in her twenties and He began to walk her through the healing of her memories. He would come to her in the night, taking her back to painful places in her childhood, where He would heal them. The death and destruction she had endured lost its power as Jesus touched her memories with His light and love.

The key principle from that day came when the session was over and all that I had heard was swirling through my brain. The magnificent ways in which Jesus had come in and out of her life since she had escaped from the occult were beyond belief. The supernatural things she had been a part of in both the Kingdom of God and the Kingdom of Darkness were amazing. I will talk more specifically about the occult and how to minister to people who have experienced it in a later chapter, but for now, understand that God used this woman and her story to teach and train me, and to hand me a very specific key to the kingdom.

At one point I asked her, "Jesus has met you and healed you many times and in so many ways. Why are you here? Why did you come to see me?"

"Because God told me to!"

"Did He tell you why?"

"I've been listening to your CDs. I think it might have something to do with my Core. I'm not sure."

"Let's do it then," I said.

We went in prayer and took Jesus to her Core, replacing the lies and pain that had been put there so deeply through years of demonic activity. Jesus is THE way, THE truth and THE life, and He wanted to be that on every level of her soul, all the way down to the core.

As I just said, much of her childhood had been programmed by the demonic. Her ancestors had served Satan for two hundred years in blood rituals and violence. God wanted her to be more than healed. He wanted to do more than fix the broken parts. He wanted her to be free from the demons in the core of her being. Jesus came to destroy the works of the devil and bring us into abundant life. He did that for her that day. She was delivered from the ancestral ties of centuries of abuse, set free to walk in her destiny as a child of God.

It was at that point that I realized Jesus is our healer, but He gave the authority over the darkness in this world to the Church. After he was crucified, the Bible teaches that he descended into hell where he took the keys to the kingdom from Satan and returned them to His Church. He has given *us* the keys of the kingdom, the kingdom of righteousness, peace, and joy. We are the ones who are responsible to remove chaos from the core of our being so we can walk right with God, and help others do the same.

We prayed through everything, and I watched as Jesus brought her even more inner healing, setting her free . She clapped her hands and laughed and cried out as we sent those demons to the pit. "I'm free. I'm finally and completely free!"

After she left my house that day, I was in awe of the Lord but I was confused.. Knowing all that God had done in her life before I saw her, I asked Him, "Why did You bring her here? You have healed so many things in her life. Why here? Why me?"

God said, *I have given* you *authority over the enemy.* He sent her to me so that I could use MY authority to send the enemy back to where he belongs. I realized then that the keys were in my hands and I needed to use that authority to bring freedom to the souls He would bring to me. Authority is another key to the kingdom that I have learned to use.

I became great friends with that woman, and God taught me many things through our friendship. She eventually had her own ministry and traveled extensively, teaching and preaching and healing people. She even had a school where she trained people to see into the supernatural. She was a powerful woman of God who knew Jesus more intimately than most people I had ever known.

I have learned many keys of the kingdom as I have walked with the brokenhearted and watched Jesus heal and restore them. Finding dead places in people's souls and bringing them back to life is one of them. Releasing people from decades of demonic oppression is another. We have authority over death and its power, but so few of us ever use it!

So few of us ever even try to learn it.

And these signs shall follow them that believe; In my name shall they cast out devils; they shall speak with new tongues; they shall take up serpents; and if they drink any deadly thing, it shall not hurt them; they shall lay hands on the sick, and they shall recover (Mark 16:17-18, KJV).

———~mᵒᵒᴄᴇᴛᴏ᷍ᴏᴛᴇᴏᴏ᷍m———

A few years into ministering to people, the Lord changed the way I would begin. He started having me bind the enemy before I did anything else, rather than wait for the demonic to manifest. If I had authority, He taught me, I could handle it up front, so I began opening with this powerful prayer:

In the name of Jesus, I bind principalities and powers, rulers, dominions, authorities and thrones and everything from the demonic realm that has been set against us. I remove all curses and devices from the Kingdom of darkness. I silence, bind, and separate from us everything that the Enemy has set against us from before the foundation of time.

This was a huge key, because it took away the enemy's ability to manifest. That made it much less painful for the people I was praying with.

For if you possess these qualities in increasing measure, they will keep you from being ineffective and unproductive in your knowledge of our Lord Jesus Christ (2 Peter 1:8, NIV).

A couple showed up for marriage counseling one day. I had led the woman to Jesus a few days before and she asked me for help with their marriage. She had met her husband online and was finding out that much of what he had told her wasn't true.

It was in the evening, and I was tired after a long day of teaching five-year-olds. I sat at the kitchen table with them and asked them what they needed. Almost immediately the man began to cry and tell me things that had happened in his childhood. When I said, "Let's talk about your marriage," he began to physically squirm. I realized that a demon was about to take over this marriage counseling session!

That's when I remembered I had forgotten to open the session with the prayer God had given me. I looked at the demon manifesting through this man and said, "I bind and silence you in the name of Jesus."

He was immediately quiet but started writhing in his chair. Then he slid off his chair and slithered his way across the living room floor. It had been years since I had seen a demonic manifestation, because I had learned to shut down the demonic before I began! When he got to the carpet he started to choke and gag. That's when I had had enough. I said, "Oh no you don't! You will not throw up on my carpet! Come out of him now!" Immediately he sat up in his right mind.

"How did I get over here?" he asked, confused.

"Does this sort of thing happen often?" asked his surprised wife.

"No, ma'am, it does not. But it's always exciting to watch God work!"

The next morning, I asked Jesus what that was all about. He gently said, *Whatever you bind is bound.*

> *I will give you the keys to the Kingdom of Heaven.*
> *Whatever you bind on Earth will be bound in*

Heaven and whatever you loose on Earth will be loosed in Heaven (Matthew 16:19, NIV).

I realized I'd silenced and bound the enemy in the man, and he was bound from his shoulders to his ankles. All he could do was slither across the floor, unable to speak or move freely until I commanded the demon to leave. I began to believe, all the more, that we have authority over demons. That demon had to do exactly what I said, even though I didn't fully understand what I was saying. I learned to do more than bind the demons. I learned to silence them, to separate them, and to shut them and their effects down completely. It saved me time, and it saved my carpet!

We have been given all authority over death and the demonic! When Jesus descended into Hell, He returned and handed us the keys to the kingdom. It is up to us to use them to unlock doors.

The Gates of Hell: Lies

It is no secret that this world is not the way God intended it to be. Everywhere we turn there is addiction, suicide, depression, violence, dishonesty, poverty, perversion, and the list goes on – seemingly - forever. Yet the Bible tells us that "the gates of Hell shall not prevail."

I remember reading this passage and saying, "But, God, the gates of Hell *are* prevailing." He told me very clearly to read it again, and to keep reading it until I came into full agreement with His Word.

He said to them, "But who do you say that I am?" Simon Peter replied, "You are the Christ, the Son of the living God." And Jesus answered him, "Blessed are you, Simon Bar Jonah! For flesh and blood has not revealed this to you, but my Father who is in heaven. And I tell you, you are Peter, and on this rock, I will build my church, and the gates of Hell shall not prevail against it" (Matthew, 16:15-19 ESV).

I eventually aligned myself with what God was saying, not with what I was seeing and hearing. Once I aligned with the truth, I asked the Lord to teach me more about the gates of Hell. What are they, and how are they opened to give the enemy access to us? And, most importantly, how could I be trained to close them?

A 'gate' is defined in Webster's Dictionary as: 'A means of entrance or exit.' A gate is an opening through which things can go in and out. Gates are mentioned many times in the Bible, and I came to learn that they are openings in the spirit realm. They give us access to either the Kingdom of Light or the Kingdom of Darkness, and give those kingdoms access to us. There are gates to Glory as well as gates to Hell. The Lord led me to four gates that need to be closed in people's souls in order to shut off access to the enemy. I began to see over and over again how these four gates had been opened to allow the enemy to wreak havoc. If we close the gates to the enemy, and open all of our gates to Jesus, HE has the freedom and access to move in with His abundant life! This has become a foundational principle in Beth Shalom.

> *Jesus said: "I am the gate. Anyone who goes through me will be cared for; will freely go in and out and find pasture. A thief is only there to steal, kill and destroy. I came so that they can have real and eternal life, more and better life than they ever dreamed of" (John 10:9;10, MSG).*

The first gate He taught me about was what I would consider "The Gate of Lies." God showed me over and over again that when people agree with a lie, it opens their soul to the devil, who is the father of lies. He can walk through the gate of lies and torment a person's soul. I often would say to people, "Tell me the lie, and I'll tell you the truth." All I knew at that point was that Jesus had said, *The truth will set you free* (John 8:32). There are many Scriptures about lies.

> *He (the devil) is a liar and the Father of lies (John 8:4, NIV).*

> *They exchanged the truth about God for a lie (Romans 1:25, NIV).*

Lies penetrate our lives at a subconscious level. They are often programmed into our minds at an early age. They come from parents, siblings, coaches, teachers, pastors and from friends. We end up believing things about life, about ourselves and about others that just aren't true. And what we believe, often unconsciously, affects our behavior. I learned that if I could identify the lie and replace it with the truth, lives could be restored. I knew that Jesus IS the Truth and that His Word IS true.

> *As he thinketh in his heart so he is (Proverbs 23:7, KJV).*

Many people bound by lies are good Christians who were raised in the Church. They maybe even stayed away from sin, but something got rooted that was not the truth. Maybe they believed the lie that they weren't good enough, or they were not wanted. They may have thought that bad things happened to them because God was angry, or that their illness was a test from God. They could think they were different from everyone, so something must have been wrong with them.

The enemy is very good at lies. He is the father of all lies, and he is most effective, especially with Christians, when he takes a piece of God's truth and twists it just a little bit.

One night someone new came to my Bible Study. She was dressed like a man and had a man's haircut. I introduced myself and quickly learned that she called herself a lesbian, but she had gotten saved and was now living a celibate life. She hoped I would train her in ministry so she could be effective in ministering to the gay community, as she truly had a heart for them. We all quickly loved Ronda and had the feeling she would be part of us as a family. A few weeks, later she asked for a ministry session with me. When I asked her what she wanted to handle in the session, she said, "I'm not sure, but I believe God will show us."

When Ronda showed up for ministry, I had her submit her will, her rights and all control to Jesus. She did. Then I silenced, bound, and separated everything from the kingdom of darkness from us. I asked God to bring me the part of Ronda that could tell me her story. When I asked what came to her mind, she shared a strange memory.

"I have this memory from time to time. I'm falling, and everything is dark. I fall and bump, fall and bump, and I can't see anything at all."

This was a recurring memory for Ronda that made no sense. She had once shared this with someone who told her it might be a memory from the womb, so had asked her mother if anything traumatic happened during her pregnancy. Her mother revealed that when she was seven months pregnant, her husband pushed her down a flight of stairs in a fit of rage, trying to kill both her and the baby. Her mother divorced him at once, never saw him again, and had Ronda as a single mother. She remarried before Ronda was two years old, and that man became her father. Neither Ronda nor her mother ever heard from her birth father again.

"Ronda came from the womb different," her mother would say. "She grew up wanting to protect everyone. She felt she had to protect girls from boys. In Junior High, she found herself watching the boys so they wouldn't harm the girls. She realized other girls were looking at boys differently than she was." It was at that age that she began calling herself a lesbian.

When I met Ronda, she was in her early fifties. She had married a woman and they had adopted children, but were no longer happy together and divorced. She believed it was better for the children not to be around their fighting. Since then, she had met Jesus and was now searching out healing.

After she told me her story, we began to pray. She invited Jesus –the Way, the Truth, and the Life –to enter her inmost being. He stepped right into that memory of falling and bumping in darkness just as we began to pray. Her eyes popped open and she said, "I've believed a lie my whole life. I've believed that I'm a lesbian, but that's not the truth!

"I wasn't attracted to boys," she continued, "and I always felt like I could protect the girls." 'Lesbian' was the only word she knew to explain how and why she was different, and the enemy twisted that and used it to make Ronda believe that this was who she was created to be. She grew up believing that was the explanation for why she felt like she needed distance from men, and why she had such a strong, protective pull toward women. This was the lie. The *truth* was that the trauma she had experienced in the womb had left her soul wanting to get away from her dad, and to love and protect and bond with her mother, who was fighting so hard to keep Ronda safe.

Ronda was never attracted to women and never wanted to have sex with them. She just wanted to love them and protect them from harm. Everything in her life had been based on a lie planted in her from the womb, when her dad tried to kill her mom. She had been hurt by him, and other men later, and she didn't want other women to be hurt by men.

We prayed through all the memories with God's healing love and forgiveness. She became aware of the way lies affected her decisions and her relationships. She has pursued God and His truth and healing for many years now. I have watched the Lord change so many things in her, inside and out. She has beautiful curly hair and a whole new wardrobe. She loves it when a man holds a door open for her. She is praying for her children and raising them to know God. She's even praying that God will bring her a husband. She's running after the goodness of God. Jesus, the Truth Himself, invaded her inmost being and turned that lie, and her life, around in a matter of minutes.

The truth will set you free (John 8:32, NIV).

I have had countless people in front of me whose whole lives have crumbled from believing a lie. If God says, "I want truth in your innermost parts," then the enemy must want to plant lies there. Ronda is one of hundreds of stories I could tell you, and there are many others in this book. We must know the truth of God so deeply that we are easily able to identify lies and SHUT that gate and cut off the access to the kingdom of darkness!

The Gates of Hell: Sin

The second gate the Lord showed me was Sin. Having grown up in the Church, I knew the devil could come in if I had sin in my life. I wish I'd been taught how to deal with sin and known that in Christ there is no condemnation. I wish I'd known that Jesus has forgiven all my sin and taken away the guilt associated with it as well. Instead, I was taught to live in fear of sin and hell, even though Jesus says again and again not to be afraid.

Then I acknowledged my sin to you and did not cover up my iniquity.

I said, "I will confess my transgressions to the Lord."

And you forgave the guilt of my sin (Psalm 32:5, NIV).

No one who lives in Him keeps on sinning. 1 John 3:6 (NIV)

One of the last things Jesus said to his disciples after He had risen from the dead, was this:

If you forgive anyone's sins, their sins are forgiven; if you do not forgive them, they are not forgiven (John 20:23, NIV).

As I have walked people through the forgiveness of sin (both their own sins and sins done against them), I have seen chains fall off. The power we have over sin is amazing, and much greater than I learned in church growing up.

But you are a chosen people, a royal priesthood, a holy nation, God's special possession, that you may declare the praises of Him Who called you out of darkness into His wonderful light (1 Peter 2:9, NIV).

If the Word is true, and we are priests and part of a royal priesthood, it is our responsibility to forgive sins. We must make forgiveness of sin part of our daily lives to overcome this sin gate. As priests, we have the power to forgive sin in the lives of others, as well as in our own life.

One day, a friend called and asked me to see a girl from her office, Valerie, who was going through some hard times. I set up an appointment with Valerie and when she came to see me, we began with prayer. As soon as I finished praying, she started crying and pouring out her heart.

Valerie had a traumatic childhood. She was conceived outside of wedlock, putting her under a curse of illegitimacy. Her mom and dad fought over her until her mother gave up and moved away, tired of seeing her precious daughter pulled back and forth. Her daddy spent his time in bars, leaving her with her grandmother. When she was nine, her father was shot and killed in a bar fight. So Valerie grew up without her father or her mother. She became pregnant as an unwed teenager. She then married Stephen, who enlisted in the military, and they began their life. They had a second child, but their marriage was never peaceful. They fought all the time, and began to grow apart.

Valerie told me she was now having an affair, as was her husband. Their teenage daughter was in trouble. What affected her most was that her youngest son, on entering Kindergarten, had been diagnosed with autism. She said he still wasn't speaking at five years old. When I asked why she came to see me, she said through her tears, "I'm a Christian and I know better! Look at this mess I've made!"

I began to talk to her, counsel her and pray with her. She got deliverance and healing that night and began to live for God. "If you will walk with God, your son will be healed," I told her.

She and her husband were living separately. She stopped her affair and for the next nine months grew in the Lord and did everything He called her to do. One night, she came to see me to say that she had changed, but her husband had not, and she was tired of waiting. It was very hurtful to see him with another woman and she wanted a divorce. She needed $800 to file for divorce and she didn't have it. So we took up an offering at our little Bible Study group. The group was amazed when they counted exactly $800 in the offering plate!

The next day, before filing for divorce, she called her husband and told him what she was planning to do. He asked where she had gotten the $800 to file and she told him her Bible Study group had taken up an offering. He asked her if "this lady" Valerie kept talking about could see him before she filed. She called me that day to set up an appointment.

As Stephen sat in front of me that evening, I asked him what he wanted from me. He said he had seen a great change in his wife; she seemed happy and at peace, and he wanted that, too. I told him the change was because of Jesus.

"I don't believe in Jesus. Is there anything else you can do for me? Will it work if I don't believe in Jesus?"

He went on to say he was raised a Jehovah's Witness, and since then he had come to the place where he didn't believe there was a God. Now he was an atheist. I told him it didn't matter what he believed. God is real. All he needed to do was to submit himself to God. Whether he believed or not didn't change the fact that God is real, and He loved him.

I led him in prayer and had him submit his will, his rights, and all control to Jesus Christ. I bound and separated the enemy from him. When I opened my eyes, he was weeping. "What's going on?" I asked.

"He's here. Jesus is here. I can see Him standing right in front of me."

"What's He saying to you?" I asked.

"He's just standing there with His arms open to me."

"You just need to receive Him," I said, and I led him in a prayer. He gave his life to Jesus that day. He repented of his sins and went home with his wife that night. They've been walking together with Jesus since that day. The fighting stopped and they learned to love each other and become the parents they needed to be.

Four years went by and Valerie got a call from her son's school. They wanted to meet with her and Stephen so that the teacher and the department head could both apologize. They said they had never had a child diagnosed with autism who was later placed in a regular class, but their son no longer needed special help and would be transferred. Jesus had healed him! He was the only child in the district ever to be moved from Special Ed. back into regular classes.

When we have sin in our lives, we create an open door for the enemy to bring chaos into our lives and relationships. When we forgive ourselves and forgive each other, sin loses its power to break in and destroy our homes. It shuts the gate of access to the enemy, and we are free and empowered to make different choices. We can choose to stop sinning.

At the Cross, Jesus paid the debt for all the sin of the world. We need to receive that forgiveness and apply His shed blood over all our sins, and those who sin against us, so we can walk in the freedom he purchased for us. If there is an impossible situation in your life, start looking for things to forgive. Choose to stop sinning and ask forgiveness for anything and everything you can think of. Things will begin to shift.

The Gates of Hell: Iniquity

The third gate God taught me about was Iniquity. Iniquity is sin that has been passed down through a family line. Sins that are not forgiven are still there, becoming generational. The King James Bible says they are 'retained.' If someone dies and no one has forgiven the sin, it is retained. It's still there and the Bible teaches that it will be passed down to three or four generations until someone forgives it or asks God to forgive it. You can see these patterns being repeated in families.

> *You shall not bow down to [idols] or worship them;*
> *for I, the Lord your God, am a jealous God, pun-*
> *ishing the children for the sin of the parents to the*
> *third and fourth generation of those who hate me,*
> *but showing love to a thousand generations of those*

who love me and keep my commandments (Exodus 20:4-6, NIV).

The world tells us we have genetic tendencies, that things like addiction, alcoholism, anger, poverty, and illegitimacy are somehow passed down through our bloodlines. When people say things like, "All the men in my family are drunks," that is not genetic . . . it is iniquity. Or, "No marriages in my family last," it is a pattern of generational sin that has never been handled. The Bible is clear that these things have a legal right to be present until the precious Blood of Jesus is applied to each damaged area. Then the love of God is visited on us and on our descendants. It is not genetic. It is spiritual and it must be handled in the Spirit. As we pray through past generational sins, we see people completely set free and their generational patterns finally broken!

I had a woman come to see me who had driven from Idaho to Texas, because she wanted to deal with her anger. She told me she was so angry with her husband that she was having images of horrible, violent acts toward him. She was a Christian and did not want to have violent, murderous thoughts flashing through her mind, but could not seem to stop them. She had been through prayer and deliverance and tried everything she knew about when a friend told her about Beth Shalom, so she called me and made her way to Texas.

As we were talking about her life, the Lord had me ask if anyone in her family line had ever killed anyone or gone to prison for violence or murder. She looked at me and asked, "Have you ever heard of the Hatfields and McCoys?"

"Yes, I have." In fact, I had just watched the TV series of how horrible and vengeful they were through several generations.

"I'm a Hatfield!"

Suddenly, it all made sense. This woman had been battling generational iniquity that had been passed down to her. We began to repent for the horrible things her family had been involved with during that terrible feud. After a bit, the anger and rage began to leave her body. She was able to forgive her husband. All the crazy images were gone. She left free of anger, no longer tormented by images of violence and bloodshed. We took all rights away from the enemy to torment her with images and thoughts of violence, and we applied the Blood of Jesus over the door of her heart. We forgave all her sins and the sins of her family that had come before her and applied it to all the generations that would follow.

———————

I met with another young woman who had been conceived out of wedlock. Her father had been the product of an affair, and had also been conceived out of wedlock. He also cheated on her mother from the time she was in the womb. He was a violent alcoholic, and her childhood had revolved around her father's drinking and cheating. She was now twenty-four years old, unmarried, and had two very young children who had each been conceived out of wedlock.

She came to see me because she didn't want to live anymore. Her life was a black hole of sadness and loneliness. She had been in several relationships that involved drugs, alcohol, violence, and cheating. She wanted to die because all she did was drink and cry. "I'm doing the same things my dad did, and I hated him for it."

We submitted to God, bound and separated the demons, and went to the inmost part of her soul in prayer. There she saw the image of a man. God was showing her that she had tried to fill her life with men. She was born illegitimate, desperate for the love and attention of her father. She had never felt worthy without the attention of a man. She repented of her past relationships and sins, for repeating the patterns of broken families, adultery, and illegitimacy that had come before her, and light began to fill that dark hole in her soul. We forgave her parents for conceiving her out of wedlock and broke the curse of illegitimacy from her life and the lives of her children. We prayed that the King of Glory would come in through every gate in her soul.

> *Lift up your heads, you gates; lift them up, you ancient doors, that the King of glory may come in.*
>
> *Who is he, this King of glory? The Lord Almighty— he is the King of glory (Psalm 24: 7-10, NIV).*

She repented of her sins and forgave everyone who had sinned against her. Then she forgave the iniquity that had been passed down to her through her family bloodlines. She said she felt like her soul was filled with "sparkling lights". All the sadness was gone.

> *But unto you who revere and worshipfully fear My name shall the Sun of Righteousness arise with heal- ing in His wings and His beams, and you shall go forth and gambol like calves [released] from the stall and leap for joy (Malachi 4:2, AMPC).*

We prayed that the Son of Righteousness would release His light into every cell in her body, soul, and spirit. We prayed He would heal her memories and her emotions. She asked God to pull down all the walls she had created through lies, sin, and iniquity. We prayed that the God Who is holy and whole would make her holy and whole, putting her back together.

> *May God himself, the God who makes everything holy and whole, make you holy and whole, put you together—spirit, soul, and body—and keep you fit*

for the coming of our Master, Jesus Christ. The One who called you is completely dependable. If He said it, He'll do it (Thessalonians 5:23-24, MSG).

She left, resolved to live the rest of her life God's way. She was determined to raise her children to know God instead of alcohol, adultery, and violence. And after we repented and forgave the iniquity in her bloodline that day, her children and their children were freed from the curses she inherited.

Sometimes people argue with me over iniquities. They say, "Jesus forgave all my sin when I got saved. And my parents were Christians, so their sins were forgiven too." The Church has not done a good job teaching us about iniquity. Most people can't even tell you what it is. The bottom line is that sin and iniquity are two different things, and Jesus paid for it all.

[Jesus] was wounded for our transgressions and bruised for our iniquities. The punishment that brought us peace was on Him and by His wounds we are healed (Isaiah 53:5, NIV).

Jesus made provision for all our sins and iniquities through His wounds at the cross. We must go to the cross and access our forgiveness by repenting for our sin and forgiving those who have sinned against us. We can also cleanse our bloodlines by repenting for the sins of our ancestors. Until the blood of Jesus is applied to all our transgressions, iniquities and wounds, they are still there, opening up gates of hell in our lives. Through repentance and forgiveness, we cancel the access that hell has in our lives. We remove all legal rights the enemy may have, and the gates of hell will not prevail.

The Gates of Hell:
Trauma

The fourth "gate of hell" is the Gate of Trauma. We all know that people are changed following a traumatic event. Marriages often break up after the death of a child or a financial crisis. Trauma can be caused by catastrophic events such as hurricanes, floods, or earthquakes. I have learned that any jolting experience can damage the souls of God's people. Divorce, adultery, illness, eviction, molestation, rape, broken bones, abuse, wrecks, accidents, broken relationships and betrayal are some of the examples of traumatic events that can damage us.

When something traumatic happens in our lives and a part of us fractures in order to handle it, we begin to respond differently to situations. Fear, doubt, unbelief, panic and even terror come into our minds; we begin to think things we would never have thought before the event, and it becomes harder to trust God. But the Bible says,

"Nothing can separate us from the love of Christ" (Romans 8:35-39, NIV).

There is nothing that happens in this world that can separate us from the love of God, not even when we feel broken and lost after a traumatic event. In a Beth Shalom session, we go right to the trauma and open the gates to the King of Glory. As the Lord enters the fractured area of the soul, our emotions and memories are immediately healed.

> *But unto you who revere and worshipfully fear My name shall the Sun of Righteousness arise with healing in His wings and His beams, and you shall go forth and gambol like calves [released] from the stall and leap for joy, (Malachi 4:2, AMPC).*

I have seen cancer, diabetes, Hepatitis C, insomnia, night terrors, Lupus and countless other horrible conditions disappear after we walk through traumatic events with Jesus. He is our Healer.

While teaching a conference in Atlanta, Georgia, a woman came up to me who had been listening to our CDs and had given a set of the CDs to her daughter. The daughter often visited a friend in a nursing home, and one day discovered the friend had a new roommate. She said to him, "You look very young to be here. How old are you?"

"I'm forty and I've gone blind and don't know how to take care of myself. I'm here to learn how to function as a blind man."

"I'm so sorry," she responded. "What happened to make you go blind?"

"They don't know. They can't figure it out."

"How long has this been going on?"

"Two years," the forty-year-old said.

Having listened to my CDs, the young woman asked, "What was going on in your life two years ago?"

"I was going through a very nasty divorce. It was awful. Then this," he said, pointing up at his cloudy eyes.

"Can I pray with you?" she asked. She had listened to me teach on what trauma does to our souls and bodies and knew this sudden blindness was not a coincidence. As people, we make up explanations in the natural to explain things in the spirit that we don't understand. We have sayings like, "When it rains, it pours." The truth is, though, trauma opens up gates in our souls and in our bodies and the effects, though they can feel unrelated, have legal ground to torment us.

This young woman in her twenties prayed for the healing of the broken soul of the man. She prayed that God would heal his broken heart and the trauma of losing his wife. She had him forgive his ex-wife. He prayed along with her and when they both opened their eyes, he could see again! His sight was completely restored! The young man's soul had been shattered through a traumatic divorce. He was so wounded and lost, his body literally registered that he was walking in darkness. Proverbs says that things going on in our lives mirror what's happened to our heart or soul.

This young woman had been learning how to ask questions. She pulled down the authority that had stolen his vision and got hold of the Shalom of God, and a blind man was healed and restored! Our purpose on the earth is to do what Jesus did, and He came to restore our souls.

> *He restores my soul. He leads me in the paths of righteousness for His name's sake (Psalm 23:3, NKJV).*

As we've already seen, trauma can begin in our lives even before we are born. My oldest brother Paul was the first-born in our family. When my mother went into hard labor with him, Daddy had to call an ambulance to get her to the hospital because Paul was a breech baby, and very large. The ambulance medics tried everything to slow her labor, but by the time they arrived at the hospital, she was in bad shape. The doctor didn't know if he could save both mother and baby, so asked my dad which one he should save. That is a traumatic birth!

Paul weighed over ten pounds and my mother was terribly torn during delivery. She hemorrhaged so badly they had to fully sedate her. When she woke up three days later, she saw the calendar and realized she had no milk in her breast. She assumed her baby was dead. As she lay in the hospital bed, a nurse came in and asked her why she was crying.

"My baby died. I don't have any milk!"

The nurse gently explained they had dried up her milk and put her to sleep so her body could heal from the trauma. She said baby Paul was healthy, and she would go and get him for her.

Paul's difficult birth was also very traumatic for him. He nearly died in an ambulance on the way to the hospital. He pushed through tissue and bones to take his first breath, and then he was all alone and didn't see his mother for three days. This set trauma so deeply inside of him, it affected who he became. Growing up, Paul was exceptionally gifted, but was always in trouble. As far back as I can remember, it seemed like there were two of him. He was broken in two from birth. No one, including Paul, knew why he was double-minded.

Within a few years of graduating from High School, he had two lives: he was living on the streets doing drugs one day, then back in church leading worship the next. There were long periods of time when he was gone, and no one knew where. He married twice and had four beautiful children. He was loved by everyone and built good relationships when he was in his right mind, but through years and cycles of addiction lost many of those relationships. I prayed with him or for him every day. He wanted to follow God and live a clean life, but was always pulled back to the streets. He needed to be put back together and I didn't know how to help him. All I knew was that God had the power to heal.

Cooking dinner one day, Jesus spoke to me. He said very clearly, *"If you don't help your brother now, he will die on the street, and nobody will even know his name."*

I got on my knees and prayed. "God, I don't even know where to find him." I wept and begged God to bring him home. Two days later, my brother called me. He and his family moved in with my family and lived with us for three months. He went cold-turkey off all drugs and was violently sick for days. He started going to church with us, made new friends, got a job, and moved his family into a cute little house. Everything seemed perfect.

Just as he began a new chapter in his life, though, I got a visit from the police. Paul's body had been found in his car and they wanted me to identify him. It didn't seem real. How could he be dead at thirty-five years old? He was finally on track and happy! He'd fought hard to get clean and get back in a right relationship with Jesus and his family.

The autopsy report said he had the body of an eighty-year-old man and his heart had just given up. Years of drugs and living on the street had cut his life short. As I look back on that time now, I see God's redemption more than I see all the pain and loss. I thank God my brother didn't die on the streets alone with broken relationships with his wife and children. He died leaving his wife and children in a home with memories of their daddy being there with them, knowing he had fought his way back.

When I got past the anger, I could see the relationships God had restored during the months Paul was with us. The day before he died, he was restless and in pain, but no one knew his heart was about to give out. He had come by to see me and I said, "Paul, what is it? What do you want?"

"To be in the Courts of the Lord," he said. I know that God heard him and the next day, Paul was worshipping his Savior in the Courts of Heaven.

This, of course, was not the deliverance and healing I had hoped for. As I grow in the Lord, I'm learning to trust that God heals and puts us back together even if we don't understand the details. I've learned many things as I've walked with Jesus about His love and grace. I wish I had known better how to bring healing into my brother's life. I didn't know then how to heal the trauma that had taken root in Paul from his birth. His life could have been so different.

Wisdom and knowledge often come through hindsight. I thank God that when I meet broken men and women now, I am equipped to bring the healing power of God to their lives. My brother was a broken man from birth. His life was divided and confused, and I believe most of it came from the trauma he experienced in the first moments of life that no one knew how to address or heal.

But now I know how to heal trauma!

Years later, after I'd learned more about the gate of trauma, I got a call from a friend on New Year's Eve. "Will you minister to my brother-in-law? He's homeless. He's been living on the street for twenty-five years as a drug addict. He's had two marriages and lost them both. He has burned everybody he knows, and no one will take him in anymore. My husband told him he can no longer live with us, so when he calls, we go and take him to lunch and see what he needs. But then we leave him on the streets. It's just killing me. I know Jesus wants to heal him." I told her to bring him to me as soon as she could, and he came the following day, on New Year's Day. They'd found him on the streets in San Antonio and driven him to me.

I learned that his father had abandoned him when he was small. His mother remarried a cruel man who beat him and threw him into walls. Often, he went without food for days at a time. He was constantly ordered to work, treated like a slave. That was his terrible life, and his mother did nothing to stop it.

One night when he was nine, his stepfather got drunk and came after him. He grabbed him by his belt, picked him up in the air and swung him down onto the hard, concrete floor. Everything cracked and the pain was blinding.

"I didn't know my back was broken," he told me. "But I knew I couldn't make a sound or he would come after me again. I waited until he was asleep and crawled over to my bed. I fell asleep, woke up the next day, and went to school. I had no choice."

He was in constant pain in school and couldn't sit still. His teacher said he should be medicated and they started him on Ritalin. Pretty soon, it didn't help. By Junior High, he was smoking weed. Soon that didn't help. By the time he was in High School, he was stealing pills and was in intense pain every minute of his life. He became an addict. He married and had a couple of kids, but couldn't kick drugs and lost his first wife. He lost his second wife, too, as well as his relationship with his children. Before he was thirty years old, he was living in homeless camps doing anything he could to stay high so he wouldn't hurt. Nobody had ever asked him his story before he came to see me.

Many people come for a ministry session, and we sit and listen to them for two or three hours. They thank us when they leave, saying things like, "Nobody's ever heard my story!" A lot of trauma gets healed just because someone cares enough to listen. God wants your story to be heard. But it gets even better than that.

I asked God to bring me the little nine-year-old boy who was slammed to the floor and left to die. I prayed that God would pick him up and touch his back. We prayed through and forgave and asked God to heal his soul and his body. Well, after forty years of suffering, God healed his back and he had no more pain! Within weeks, he was off the street and had a job and his own apartment. He reconciled with his children and his grandchildren. Later, he got a better job and bought a motorcycle. He now loves Jesus and has his life back. He is restored to wholeness. I saw him recently and he is doing really well.

Some people believe the lie that if God doesn't touch them, it must be their fault. No, it's not! They have been broken through trauma. Trauma is a gate from hell, but these hellish gates shall not prevail when the Church of Jesus Christ moves in the Authority He gave us.

> *I have given you authority to trample on snakes and scorpions and to overcome all the power of the enemy; nothing will harm you (Luke 10:19, NIV).*

God is the healer, and He wants to shut the Gates of Trauma in our lives that have given the enemy access to us. And He wants to heal us from every effect of that trauma in our souls and in our bodies.

Beth Shalom

In the early years of ministry, I was amazed at how many people commented on the peace they felt in our home. I heard comments like, "I came by to talk but you weren't here, so I just sat on the porch. It was so peaceful, and I feel better now. I don't think I need anything else." I thought every home felt like that.

One time, a group of teenagers came from Houston for a weekend retreat. My middle brother thought it would be good to bring kids from the big city to spend some time with God in the country. The day they arrived, though, our air conditioner went out. It was so hot we couldn't do anything inside the house. The kids slept outside on the deck and under the trees. I thought these poor kids probably couldn't wait to get back to their air-conditioned homes! Texas in the summer with no AC can feel like living in an oven. On the final day, their pastor told them to find a place to be with God and let Him talk to them about the weekend. Then they were to write down what He showed them. One of the girls made a card for me with the word that God had given her. It was Isaiah 32:15-20. Verse 20 speaks of a place where even the animals are free:

> *How blessed you will be, Sowing your seed by every stream, And letting your cattle and donkeys range free (Isaiah 32:20, NIV).*

This young girl had helped raise horses, and she was amazed that our horse was not in a fenced area. The horse, Levi, belonged to my daughter Jenny. We had a small corral for him, but it seemed silly to keep him fenced in all day when we had so much land. Jenny would go out in the morning and feed him and leave the gate open so he could graze wherever he liked. We had no idea this wasn't a good idea, and Levi always stayed close to the house. He wanted to be where the children were. If we were inside, he would come up on the deck and push his nose against the back door until someone shared a snack with him. He especially liked chocolate chip cookies!

One of my favorite memories is watching my six-year-old son, James, climb all over him as he lay in the grass. We had a saddle, but Jenny and Levi preferred bareback riding. She would hop on his back and head for the meadow down by the creek. Sometimes I would see two or three of my children on Levi at the same time, heading off for adventures beyond.

It was years before I realized that the peace and freedom we enjoyed so much in our home and on the land were special blessings from Heaven. We were all like Levi, ranging free on the land and enjoying the peace of God. God was teaching me how important peace is.

> *My people will live in peaceful dwelling places, in secure homes, in undisturbed places of rest. Though hail flattens the forest, and the city is leveled com-*

pletely, how blessed you will be, sowing your seed by every stream, and letting your cattle and donkeys range free (Isaiah 32:18-20, NIV).

———～ᴡ∘∘ᴇ𝕏∘̂𝕏∘∘ᴡ———

One Saturday morning my friend Gary asked me to meet him at my church to pray for his friends. They had driven three and a half hours from Dallas, and Gary had promised them God would heal both of them if I prayed for them. No pressure!

Gary's friend suffered from severe anxiety. He'd been to the hospital several times for panic attacks. So many times, in fact, they were now having financial problems from all the Emergency Room visits. The doctors said it was anxiety, but could not seem to do anything that helped him.

He had been married for fifteen years and his wife was barren. They were desperate and Gary had promised them healing. I was upset he had promised these things and put me on the spot. I prayed all the way to the church, "Jesus, please show up!" I knew I had nothing to give this couple unless Jesus came. Now *I* was the one who was anxious!

I met Gary in the nursery at church to wait for the couple. His phone rang and he went outside for better reception. As soon as he stepped out of the room, I felt Jesus step in. His precious presence permeated the atmosphere of that little nursery. I was so relieved that He had come. When Gary came back into the room, he knew I was different.

"What happened?" he said.

"Jesus is here!"

The couple arrived and we prayed together. Jesus showed us everything we needed to know to pray effectively for both of them, and they were completely healed! The man is now free from anxiety and has an online ministry praying worldwide with people who suffer as he did. Within months his wife conceived, and they now have several children.

Jesus showed up!

The cool part for me, aside from seeing God move in power, was that at the end of the session I asked the man if he was feeling or seeing or sensing anything from the Lord.

"I keep seeing a house. It's out in the country, surrounded by corn fields. It's blue and has a wraparound porch."

"Monte, that's your house!" Gary said. This man had no idea where I lived or what my house looked like. I knew God was talking to me through him.

"Go up on the porch and tell me what you see," I directed.

"The door is white and has an oval glass in it. There's a sign above the door that says, 'Beth Shalom.'"

That was the first time I ever heard those words. *Beth Shalom.* I knew God was talking to me about all He had called me to do. He was putting a name to it and calling it His own. I studied and learned that 'Beth' is Hebrew for a place, dwelling, or house. I had heard that 'Shalom' meant 'peace.' God was saying my home was a place of peace. He had a plan for my ministry, and He called it Beth Shalom. I was so excited. I began to call everything God did through me "Beth Shalom." Whatever was going on with a person, my job was to bring him or her to a place of peace.

Time passed and Beth Shalom expanded. People came more frequently from other cities. A family from Austin brought their son to pray with me and Jesus set him free! They had taken him to other ministries and no one could help. They had begun to lose hope and feared that they had lost their child.

The young man was fifteen and he didn't want to live. He told his parents he wanted to die, but they had no idea why. He was in a good Christian family and church. He had friends and good health. Everything in his life seemed fine, but every night he was tormented. We prayed and God revealed that he had memories from the womb of things his mother felt while she carried him. As he forgave everything, the torment left and we all knew he was free. Jesus healed him and we were all amazed.

More people came from Austin, many of them involved with inner healing. They came to me wanting ministry and training. I remember a woman asking me what was different about Beth Shalom from other healing ministries, and what I did that other ministries weren't doing. I had no idea what they did or didn't do! It seemed to me I was the only one who had no formal training, and I'd always just asked God to teach me.

One woman told me that someone from Bethel, a well-known church in California, had done a teaching at her church on the "Shalom of God." She learned that the word *Shalom* means much more than just peace. It means, "Nothing Missing, Nothing Broken, and the Absence of Chaos." That was key for me. I knew my ministry was not only about healing wounds. It was about removing the chaos and demons from people's lives. We had to do both simultaneously to attain real freedom.

As I taught other ministers, I realized many of them knew nothing about the authority the Church has over demons and the devices of hell. So, I began to teach on the gates of hell and how to stand in the authority of Christ. For years I had felt that my calling was to awaken the Church to move in more authority. Now I was doing it.

On this rock I will build my church, and the gates of hell shall not prevail against it. Matthew (16:18b, NIV).

As the ministry grew, so did my understanding of what God intended when He wrote "Beth Shalom" over the door of my home. Years into Beth Shalom, a woman from Georgia came for a session. At the end, she asked me if I knew what *Shalom* meant. I immediately knew God was about to give me another piece.

"I think so, but tell me," I said.

She went on to explain that every symbol in Hebrew has its own meaning. They are much more than our English letters. Each symbol has a deep meaning. When you put the four symbols together that spell *shalom'* in Hebrew, the true, deep meaning means, "the power to destroy every authority that binds chaos."

I had learned how to find the missing pieces in a person's life, to put back together what was broken and to deal with demonic torment. Learning that *shalom* meant "nothing missing, nothing broken and the absence of chaos," was a major part of that. Then this woman who had studied Hebrew revealing that it meant that I have the power to destroy every demonic authority that tries to bind chaos to a life… I knew God had chosen the perfect name for the ministry.

Beth Shalom.

"Shalom Aleikhem!" Yeshua repeated. "Just as the Father sent me, I myself am also sending you" (John 20:21, CJB).

Mexico

After Bible study one night my friend, Dorciane, who became one of my closest companions and ministry partners, got a phone call from the son of one of her dearest friends. She was upset and asked if I would go and pray for her friend. The friend wasn't eating or sleeping, and her children had put her in a mental hospital. They didn't know what to do. This had been going on for a couple of months and she wasn't improving. Dorciane asked if I would go and see her.

"Of course I'll go. Where is she?"

"Acapulco," she said. I laughed.

This was Beth Shalom's first international ministry trip! Aaron the angel had prophesied over me that I would go to hundreds of places to thousands of people. And here it was. Dorciane bought the tickets and two weeks later, we flew out.

When we arrived at the woman's beautiful home, she was clearly despondent. I got out my notebook and pen, and we went straight into her library where she began telling me her story. I could see she was fractured from the traumatic event that had occurred in her home three months earlier. There had been a suicide of a family member and she'd found the body in her upstairs bedroom. She was shattered, unable to recover.

I had her submit her will, her rights and all control to God. I bound the enemy and we invited Jesus into these shattered memories. I prayed with her about other things that also came up, and before long she was laughing and peaceful. Jesus had healed her soul.

"Are we done yet? How long are we going to pray?" she asked.

"We can stop now," I said, and I asked the Lord to remove the enemy and seal her healing.

"I bet you're hungry," she said cheerfully.

She went into the kitchen and made a big pot of shrimp soup. It was the best soup I'd had in my whole life! It's been many years now and she's had no more mental health issues. God healed her, delivered her, and put her back together. God is so good! His love for us is so amazing.

He restores my soul (Psalm 23:3, NKJV).

While we were in Acapulco, Dorciane got a phone call from her husband, Andy, who wanted us to come up to a village in the mountains. Andy had gone to visit a small church he had planted years ago. We got in the old van packed with noisy chickens and children, and every kind of produce, and took the two-hour trip up the steep, winding mountain road to the village. When we arrived, Andy took me into the church. There, we saw a woman sitting quietly. She had been at the altar for hours, waiting for us to arrive.

When I asked her if she wanted prayer, all she could say was, "I'm broken!" I told her that Jesus sent us to put the pieces of her life back together. And God put her back together that day! We discovered that she was the pastor's wife. He immediately knew that she was transformed, and he wanted that freedom for his whole church.

Through the years, many people in his church have received freedom in Christ. His church came back to life and he became a regional leader in the area. There is now a Bible School in his village where men and women are trained and ordained, taking the Gospel to other villages in the mountains.

Earlier that morning, just as my feet touched the tarmac in Mexico City, my phone rang. It was my friend Patricia who has been an intercessor for Beth Shalom Ministries for many years.

"I'm so glad I caught you. I've been praying for you. Jesus has got your back, Monte, and He's given you five 'P's – Provision, Preparation, Power, and Protection for His Purposes. These things will always be there for you. He's given you power over Legion. I'm not sure what that means, but it's very important for me to tell you that. You have been given power over Legion!"

I thanked her for the call and for all her prayers and headed to the terminal. A few days later, we were asked to visit a deliverance ministry camp where people went to get off drugs. We pulled up to the place and saw high concrete walls with razor wire along the top. There were chains and locks on the gate. We went in and saw people in shackles, bound together in twos with chains around their ankles, wandering around in a daze on the concrete floor. A few picnic tables were the only furniture to be seen.

When we met with the director, we told him we had a healing and deliverance ministry. We wanted to share what God had shown us, and to help in any way we could. The director then showed us a video of a TV commercial he had produced. It showed a high-end spa and pictures of people reclining on sofas talking to a counselor. The ad said that people could get free of drugs – for a few thousand dollars. People were sending their loved ones there, thinking this was what they would get. In reality it was worse than any prison I have ever visited or seen on TV! We felt sick inside and I wondered why God had brought us to this horrible place.

I tried once more to tell the director that God had given me tools to set people free.

"How many people do you work with?" he said.

"Usually one at a time," I explained.

"Anyone can do that! I work with thirty or forty people at a time," He bragged.

We could hardly believe the terrible things he did. He put people on buses and took them into the woods and left them there all day. He would play loud praise music and make them dance until they were in a state of hysteria. We never saw the lounge with the luxurious couches or the delicious food he promised on the promotional video.

Dorciane pressed him. "You should let Monte tell you some of the things God has shown her."

"Let's see what God has shown her," he mocked. "I'll give you one woman and we'll see what you can do!"

We didn't know at the time that this woman had been through his program three times, but was getting worse each time! A young man led Dorciane and me into a storage room where we sat on boxes in a small, crowded closet, surrounded by paper goods and plastic ware. They brought the woman in to me and she seemed to be mentally handicapped.

Dorciane translated for us and I asked the woman if she would submit her will, her rights and all control to God. She said she would, and I prayed to bind the enemy of her soul. When I opened my eyes, she looked like a different woman: this woman whom I had assumed was mentally handicapped actually had a Master's degree in Education! When I asked why she was at this place, she told me her story.

"I was watching TV one day and the news came on. My next-door neighbor had been shot in cold blood by a man from the Cartel. It was very traumatic. I was very scared and began to believe that if they killed him, they could kill me or anyone in my family. I became consumed with fear and began to have panic attacks. I stopped sleeping and lost my mind and, finally, my family sent me here. I have gotten even worse since I got here."

We prayed for her and God healed her fractured soul, delivering her from the power of the enemy. She left that closet free, laughing and clapping her hands, running and leaping and praising God, just like the man in the temple. Nothing could contain her new joy. She was healed and she knew it. Jesus had made her whole again.

> *And he took him by the right hand and raised him up: and immediately his feet and his anklebones received strength. And leaping up, he stood, and began to walk; and he entered with them into the temple, walking, and leaping, and praising God (Acts 3:7-8, ASV).*

We walked out and I could see the director was agitated that she had gotten so free, so quickly. I thought he would ask me what we had done, but he continued taunting me. "Anyone can do that with one person! Let's see what you can do with a whole group of people."

He led us into a larger room and brought in about forty people, still chained together in pairs. They sat in rows of chairs and I stood in front of them. All I saw was a group of broken, demonized people. Some were mumbling, others were shaking their heads and drooling. I knew this was "Legion."

I closed my eyes and looked up to the Heavens. I took authority over principalities and powers, rulers and dominions, authorities, and thrones and I shut down all demonic activity and communication. I bound, silenced, and separated everything that had been set against these people from the kingdom of darkness. I asked the Lord to come to that place and demonstrate His power to those men and women.

When I opened my eyes, I saw a different group of people. They were attentive and sitting up, and they were all in their right minds. We were amazed at what God had done. Then I remembered what Patricia had said to me on the phone: "He has given you authority over Legion!" Her prophecy was fulfilled.

> *When they came to Jesus, they saw the man who had been possessed by the legion of demons, sitting there, dressed and in his right mind; and they were afraid (Mark 5:15, NIV).*

I turned to Mr. Director and said, "Now sir, get these people on their feet and send them home." He didn't say a word, he just looked at us. We left that place in awe of what we had seen God do. We climbed into our vehicle. None of us could speak. We were in awe and wonder. The fear of God had come, and we had seen His power!

Someone called from a neighboring village needing our help. We were loaded into a broken-down pick-up truck and driven by a 13-year-old boy to a woman's home. She was shaking, unable to speak. She couldn't stop crying. That morning, on her way to the village to sell her cheese, a man from the Cartel had knocked her to the ground and held a machine gun to her head. For forty-five minutes he intimidated her and used her as an example of what would happen to anyone who disobeyed them. The week before, they had killed a teenage boy and hacked his body into pieces because he stayed out past curfew, working in the fields. They were controlling the people in the villages through terror.

I sat down beside the woman and asked her if she wanted Jesus to heal her. She nodded. I laid my hands on her and we began to forgive everything that happened to her that day. Dorciane translated as I asked the Lord to put her back together, to invade her memories and emotions and fill her with peace. Within minutes, she was back to herself. Shortly after praying for her, she served us delicious "street tacos" on homemade tortillas. It reminded me of the story of Jesus healing Peter's mother-in-law.

> *When Jesus came into Peter's house, he saw Peter's mother-in-law lying in bed with a fever. He touched her hand and the fever left her, and she got up and began to wait on him (Matthew 8:14,15, NIV).*

In the same village there was a man named Victorino who had been confined to bed for weeks, unable to walk. His son had come to our workshop and invited us to come and pray for his father. Victorino's feet and legs were swollen and red and it hurt to put any weight on them. The pain had begun two or three months earlier and he had become bedridden shortly after the pain began. He could hardly move at all.

I asked the Lord to show him what was going on in his life at the time this started. He was quiet at first, then the Lord reminded him he had been angry and upset with his children. He had a dozen children and only one of them was following God. He raised them to know Jesus, and he was angry that they were not walking with God the way he wanted them to. I had him repent of his anger, forgive his children, and release them to God. The Lord showed me that he was holding on to anger so deeply that it was literally affecting "his walk."

We anointed his feet and legs with oil and prayed for the Son of Righteousness to arise with healing in his wings and in his beams of Light. Then we went back down the road to our place for dinner.

The next morning, we were sitting outside the house when Victorino came walking toward us, fully dressed and on his feet. He told us God had healed him as soon as we had prayed for him. He had killed a chicken and his wife was busy making soup for us. He invited us to his home for breakfast, where we were served hot chicken soup made with fresh herbs and vegetables from his garden. His wife made homemade tortillas and served them to us as fast as we could eat them. Everything was delicious! He played his guitar and sang to us as we ate. They were both so happy he was healed. It was a precious time.

As soon as he let God cleanse his soul of anger and resentment, he was able to walk again. The body mirrors what is going on inside of us. Holding anger, resentment, and hurt in our hearts damages our emotions and affects our ability to walk as Jesus intended.

As water reflects the face, so one's life reflects the heart (Proverbs 27:19, NIV).

"In your anger do not sin." Do not let the sun go down while you are still angry, and do not give the devil a foothold, (Ephesians 4:26-27, NIV).

When we got home, after praying at the church, my friends led me upstairs to my room. We climbed up a ladder and through a trap-door in the ceiling. One side of the room had a huge glass window overlooking a garden. It was a simple room with only a bed, table, and lamp.

Many years before, Andy, Dorciane's husband and a lifelong missionary, visited the small villages in the mountains. He led one couple to the knowledge of Christ and they had walked faithfully with the Lord ever since. The woman told her husband, "I want to build a room for the prophet, so he has a place to stay when he comes to the mountains." They built a room just like the one that was built for the prophet Elijah, and it had been Andy's room for years. As time went by, other rooms were added to the house. This trip, Andy and Dorciane were staying in a room downstairs and I was given the prophet's room.

Every night, God would speak to me through my dreams. On the last morning of the trip, I dreamed that I woke up and climbed downstairs and walked into the room where Andy and Dorciane were packing their bags, getting ready to go. As I entered the room, a woman from the village came in through the front door. She was wearing, of all things, a cape. She moved to the end of the bed, lifted up the cape and laid two newborn babies on the foot of the bed: a little boy and a little girl. She spoke a few words in Spanish, which I understood in my dream.

"One is for Andy, and one is for Monte," she said.

Dorciane got all excited he said, "I can help."

In the dream, we all knew that God was birthing two ministries. The little boy represented a Bible College in the mountains. Since that time Andy has started Bible Colleges throughout the region and has been equipping pastors and leaders to spread the gospel in the area. The little girl represented our ministry, Beth Shalom.

Since that first trip to Mexico, Beth Shalom has grown and spread in both the USA and internationally. When Jesus appeared to his disciples after the Resurrection and said, "*Shalom I leave with you. My Shalom I give to you.*" He was releasing to us the power to reconcile all things to God that have been stolen or destroyed by the enemy. Shalom is the reconciliation of all things to God through the work of Christ. Shalom is physical, psychological, social, and spiritual peace. It gets you right with yourself and with God. Jesus died to set us free, so we can walk in power and authority over everything that keeps us from being all He created us to be. Whether we are ministering to a group in our home or healing a broken soul in the mountains of Mexico, this is our model for Beth Shalom Ministries.

Your hearts can soar with joyful gratitude when you think of how God made you worthy to receive the glorious inheritance freely given to us by living in the light. He has rescued us completely from the tyrannical rule of darkness and has translated us into the kingdom realm of his beloved Son. For in the Son, all our sins are canceled, and we have the release of redemption through his very blood.

He is the divine portrait, the true likeness of the invisible God, and the first-born heir of all creation. For through the Son everything was created, both in the heavenly realm and on the earth, all that is seen and all that is unseen. Every seat of power, realm of government, principality, and authority—it was all created through him and for his purpose! He existed before anything was made, and now everything finds completion in him.

He is the Head of his body, which is the church. And since he is the beginning and the firstborn heir in resurrection, he is the most exalted One, holding first place in everything. For God is satisfied to have all his fullness dwelling in Christ. And by the blood of his cross, everything in heaven and earth is brought back to himself—back to its original intent, restored to innocence again (Colossians 1:12-20, (TPT).

May God himself, the God who makes everything holy and whole, make you holy and whole, put you together—spirit, soul, and body—and keep you fit for the coming of our Master, Jesus Christ. The One who called you is completely dependable. If he said it, he'll do it (1 Thessalonians 5:23-24, MSG).

In Pursuit of His Presence: My Early Years

A s I mentioned in the Introduction of this book, I grew up in church, but was not taught the power or the presence of God. I knew nothing about the supernatural world. However, there were many times as a child that I would feel an overwhelming peace come over my body. Sometimes I would feel it pass over me in waves. Most times it was when I was alone, but as I grew older, I began to feel it in our church as well. Later, I realized that what I was feeling was the magnificent presence of God. The Lord had planted in me a desire for His presence very early on.

> *As a deer pants for the water, so my soul longs for you, oh God (Psalm 42:1, NIV)*

Even though my church didn't teach about or practice the power of God, they did teach scripture. They pounded the Word into me. We heard it, we were to memorize it. Somehow, even though they weren't really living it, I got a lot of the word hidden in my heart as a young girl. I knew the rules. "Don't do this. Don't do that, or you might go to hell." And I knew all of the Bible stories about healing and power. But I also remember that it made me question. If these things are in the Bible, why don't I see them happening today? I knew we were supposed to pray all the time, but I didn't know why, when we prayed for people, pretty much nothing happened.

My first memory of praying for the broken was when I was three years old. I grew up in Houston in the days when kids played outside all day and came in when the street lights came on. We knew that at the same time every day, a man who lived down the street would screech onto our street in his loud truck, coming home from work. When we heard it, we'd get off the street in a hurry because he would speed fast, slam on his brakes and get out of the truck. He'd cuss all the way up the driveway, slam the door and go into the house. It was that way every day. I was only three, so I didn't know he was drunk, but I remember feeling the pain and the rage in that man's heart. I wanted to help him somehow, so I prayed for him every day.

My family went to church every time the door opened. My daddy was a leader, so we were always there. I knew the rules: if somebody is sick, you pray; if somebody's mad, you pray; if somebody is bad, you pray. And so, I would pray, and I remember the Holy Spirit talking to me as the man came slamming down the street one evening. My heart was weeping, and I realized he didn't know Jesus. That's why he was so angry. Nobody had ever told him about God. So there I was at three years old – tiny, but determined! *I'm going to tell him today. If he knows that Jesus loves him, he won't feel this way anymore!*

I waited for him across the street, and soon here he came. "Cuss, cuss, cuss." He was walking and yelling and screaming, then he slammed the door and went inside. I walked onto his porch and knocked on the door. He didn't come. I knocked a little louder, and he still didn't come. Finally, I knocked as loud as I could and this great big, old man opened the door. At first, he didn't see me. I wasn't even tall enough to reach the doorknob. Then he looked down and said gruffly, "What do you want?"

"I just had to tell you: Jesus loves you." The man took his boot and shoved me away with his foot, cussing as he slammed the door. He didn't hurt me, just knocked me down. But I laid there and wept for him because I knew he was on the heart of God. There was something in me saying, "He just needs Jesus." I didn't know how to bind the enemy, or how to silence the voices in his head. I didn't know how to help him get his heart back together. All I knew was that this man needed God.

Years later, a boy named Tommy would come to our neighborhood with a can of spray paint. He sprayed it into a bag and breathed the paint to get high. One day I saw Tommy in the ditch, bagging paint, and I asked him, "Why are you doing that?"

He told me he'd been abused every day of his life, and this was the only way he knew to stop the pain in his body and in his soul. I took him to church because I knew, even at fourteen, that Jesus was this boy's answer. Jesus is the answer for addiction. He's the answer for alcoholism. He's the answer for heartache, abuse, divorce, and disease. So, I took him to the church and, sadly, it didn't turn out well. He was afraid to go home, so he started sleeping up in the balcony! The church put out a peace bond against him and he wasn't allowed on the premises. Talk about hurt, rejection and abuse! But I didn't give up.

I knew Tommy was a good guy, but I also knew he did bad things. When we would sit and talk, he would tell me stories and we'd laugh and have a good time. Five minutes later, he'd steal something from someone's garage, then get high as a kite.

I didn't get it: why were there two Tommy's? I was angry with God and thought He wasn't doing what He said he would. Later, I realized I was feeling what God was feeling – but it was the Church that wasn't doing what she should be doing. God had made the provision. He had laid it all out. It was easy. It was there. Every bit of it. The Bible says we have everything we need for life and for godliness through the knowledge of Christ.

> *Everything we could ever need for life and complete devotion to God has already been deposited in us by His divine power. For all this was lavished upon us through the rich experience of knowing Him who has called us by name and invited us to come to Him through a glorious manifestation of his goodness (2 Peter 1:3, TPT).*

I began to question everything. I needed tools but, no one in my life, including – apparently – my church, had them. For years I prayed and searched for answers. I knew God answered prayer and had the power to heal and deliver everyone. I was tired of excuses for why that wasn't happening. I wanted answers. Through the years I began to have a greater understanding of the Word of God. I realized my lack of knowledge was the biggest problem. I began to dig into His Word and beg for revelation, especially about healing and deliverance. I wanted to see people walk completely free of addiction and pain.

In the late sixties, as the Jesus Movement hit Houston, there were times when I felt His presence in meetings as I heard testimonies or music. The atmosphere would shift as people began to talk or sing about the goodness of God. I was captivated by it, but didn't have the vocabulary to describe it. I knew it was the presence of God right there with me, and I knew this was the answer for the hurt I saw around me that no one seemed to know how to handle.

As time passed, I began to understand that being in His presence felt differently and smelled differently. Things shifted in and around me. I loved going to summer camps and sitting by Peach Creek and just being still, feeling that wonderful peace sweep over me. Every time that I felt it, I would recommit my life to Him and His purposes. I felt sure that one day I would be on the mission field. I had visions of being in a canoe going down the Amazon or Nile River, going into jungles and villages with the gospel and seeing tribes of lost souls coming to Christ.

Then everything in my world fell apart. One of our church leaders had an affair with a teenager. I felt hurt, angry, and confused. I was wrestling with God and what I believed.

One night, I went out with some friends and one of them put something in my drink. When I woke up, I realized that he had stolen my virginity. My world began to spiral out of control. I was devastated. I began to believe that I was disqualified from ever serving God. Inner walls came up that kept me from feeling that peace and hearing His voice. I believed that it was all my fault and that I could never be used by God. I became very angry and hurt. Filled with shame, I withdrew from God and almost everyone else I was close to. I believed I could never be loved if anyone knew who I really was. I began to medicate my pain with alcohol.

I entered High School as a completely different person. My friend groups also changed. Now there were two people living in my body. It would be years before I understood that I had fractured from trauma and needed to be put back together. One part of me wanted to be holy and pure and save the world from darkness and sin, and the other was so hurt and angry that she had begun to deny that there even was a God.

The sweet presence of God I had experienced in my childhood became so much harder to find. My walls separated me from the One I loved most.

During my first Literature assignment at Southwest Texas State University in San Marcos, Texas, I had to write an essay on hypocrisy, based on a short story from Flannery O'Connor. Writing poured out of me. I hadn't processed the split in the church, the betrayal and confusion I felt when my leader had an affair, or how that had affected me. But here it was. I read through the first few paragraphs I had written and it hit me: It wasn't God I hated, but hypocrisy.

Immediately, I felt the presence of God fill my dorm room, and I heard the Lord speak. He said, very gently, right behind me, "So do I."

It had been several years since I'd felt his presence. It was so tender, and I was so happy to hear him again. I asked the Lord out loud, "Then I can walk with you again?"

I was free. The walls in my inside world fell down, just like at Jericho! I began to tell everyone about Jesus. My search for His presence was on again.

My roommate, Debi, told me I needed to be filled with the Holy Spirit to break free from patterns I had created to medicate my pain. On my eighteenth birthday, I went to Debi's grandmother's church. I came in late and sat by myself on the very back pew. I waited for the altar call and the invitation to receive the Baptism of the Holy Spirit. As soon as the pastor gave the call to receive, I felt the presence of God touch the top of my head and pour down my body, like a warm liquid, all the way down to my toes.

Then I heard someone say, "God wants to fill you from the top of your head to the souls of your feet."

I knew I had it now. Whatever this power was, God had poured it into me on that back pew. I had never felt the power of God move through my body before. All I could say was, "Thank you, Lord.

What do you want now? I'll serve and obey you for the rest of my life."

I heard the Lord say, "*Go down to that altar.*"

I looked to the front, where people were on the floor, babbling away, or dancing. "No way! Those people are doing crazy things!" As soon as I said it, I realized I'd literally just promised that I would obey God forever, and here I was, seconds later, arguing with Him! Reluctantly, I walked down the aisle to the altar, careful not to make eye contact with anyone. I knelt down and closed my eyes, hoping it would all go away. Debi's grandmother came and put a very shaky hand on my head and asked, "Did you receive the Baptism of the Holy Spirit with the evidence of tongues?"

I looked that woman straight in the eye and said, "Yes." I wasn't in this for "tongues." I had come for the power of the Holy Spirit. At that moment, I realized that my first act of obedience to God, after receiving the Holy Spirit, was to tell a lie at the altar! I bowed my head and asked God to forgive me. I heard Him gently say to me, "*It's okay, Monte, I've got this!*"

I wasn't sure what the baptism of the Holy Spirit or speaking in tongues was supposed to be, but I felt alive. I was hearing God's voice and feeling his presence again. I knew I was changed. I knew I would never be without His presence again. My life became an absolute pursuit of the presence of God, and has been ever since.

Bit by a Serpent

It was almost dark one evening and my first husband, Steve, was on the lawnmower. We were trying to get the lawn mown before dark. The children were playing on the trampoline, and I was trying really hard to get the yard looking good. Right at dusk, I was pulling weeds on the side of the house near the deck, and I reached in and grabbed a handful, pulled them up and threw them. I reached in again. The second time I felt something hit my hand; it was really, really painful. I threw down the handful of weeds and ran in the house to wash my hands to try and see what had happened. The pain was incredible! As I washed my hands my husband and kids came running in.

"What's the matter, Mom?"

"Something got me, but I don't know what it was."

I thought it was maybe a scorpion, but wasn't sure. All I knew was that something had stung or bitten me. My hand began to swell, and the pain was intense. One of the kids said, "Pray."

Steve took my hand and began to pray. As he prayed, the pain left, but the swelling didn't. It continued to swell bigger and bigger. My hand was two or three times the size it should be. Since it didn't hurt, though, I didn't worry about it. I got the kids in bed and went to sleep. It continued to throb and swell through the night.

Dropping the kids off at school the next morning, a friend saw my hand and asked, "What happened to you?"

"I don't know. Something got me last night when I was working in the yard."

"Have you been to a doctor?"

By now my hand was turning green and it was swollen all the way up to just past my elbow. My arm was twice the size it should be, and my hand was three times the size it should be! It was starting to feel mushy.

"You need to go to a doctor! I'll watch the kids. You go!" Two of my children were not yet in school, so she kept them and insisted I go.

Walking into my doctor's office, I didn't have an appointment so I didn't know if he would see me.

I told the receptionist, "I need to see Dr. Rogers."

"Do you have an appointment?"

"No."

"What do you need?" she asked.

When I held up my hand she shot out of her chair, went to get Dr. Rogers, and I was in his office in about twenty seconds. He very carefully looked at my hand, turned it over, and pressed on my skin right where the pain had begun. I clearly saw two little fang marks.

"What kind of snake was it?"

Snake!? I hadn't even thought of that.

"I don't know, I didn't see it. It was dark and I was pulling weeds."

"When did this happen?"

"Last night, about 6:00. What do I need to do?" I asked.

He looked at me and shook his head. "It's too late for us to do anything," he said. "We'll just have to wait and see. If you're going to take anti-venom, you have to do it within twelve hours."

I wasn't afraid. The minute he said the word "snake," I knew what the word of God said. Snakes have no power over us. We can handle them, we can even drink poison and no harm will come to us. I felt faith begin to rise up in me and I knew I would be okay because the Bible is very clear concerning snakes.

> *They will pick up snakes with their hands; and when*
> *they drink deadly poison, it will not hurt them at*
> *all; they will place their hands on sick people, and*
> *they will get well (Mark 16:18, NIV).*

———

I had a memory from years before, after I was newly married. I lived in a small Christian community where several families lived together and just pursued the things of God. We enjoyed each other's fellowship, prayed, studied, farmed and played together.

One night, Steve and I were playing dominoes with another couple when the dogs started barking outside. Bob, our friend, hollered, "Shut up, Red Dog!"

But Red Dog didn't shut up. After repeatedly telling the dog to be quiet, Bob finally got up to check on Red Dog. He stepped down off the steps, right on top of a copperhead! The copperhead bit him on the ankle. Red Dog had been trying to alert us to the snake outside the door. Red Dog was a good dog.

Bob came in, told Steve where the snake was, and Steve went out and killed it. We put ice on Bob's ankle, but it was already turning blue and purple. It looked horrible. Cindy, his wife, started packing the diaper bag (they had a newborn baby).

"What are you doing, Cindy?" he asked.

"We're going to the hospital," she stated matter-of-factly, still packing the bag.

"We're not going to the hospital. We're going to finish our game."

Cindy pleaded with him, pointing to his ankle. Bob would have none of it.

"I have based my life on the Word of God. Either it's true, or it's not. The Bible says snakes have no power over us, and if that's the truth, I'll be fine. If that's not the truth, then I don't want to live. My life is based on what God says in his Word. Now sit back down and let's finish these dominoes."

Day after day went by and he was just fine. We heard that three days later a neighbor was bitten by a copperhead and lost three of her fingers! We knew Bob's snake bite could have been terrible, but he trusted God and he was healed.

I, too, learned to trust God during the season we lived in that little community. I learned with the core of my being that we really can depend on God's Word, and we are to base our lives on what the Word of God says. *This* is what rose up in me when Dr. Rogers said "snake." Here was my chance to line my life up with the Word of God!

It was about a year before my hand was completely back to normal from that snake bite, but it never hurt. I didn't lose my fingers. I didn't lose sleep, and I never even had pain. It certainly did not look very pretty, and it turned every color of the rainbow. Everyone who saw it made a face and asked me what I was going to do about it. I would just say, "God's going to heal me."

Several times during the year I went for prayer. The first time I asked one of the elders in our church to pray. I remember him looking at my hand with a grave, expression on his face and told me it was a very serious thing. But as he put his hand on my hand, God spoke to him. Instead of praying for my hand, he began to pray about my life.

"God, teach her. Teach her how to help those who have been bitten by the serpent. Teach her how to deal with those who are wounded on the inside, those whose flesh is not as strong as it should be, those who are bruised and battered. God, use her to bind up wounded places. God, show her what happens to somebody when the enemy strikes." Through the years, those words have come back again and again as I see someone in front of me who's been bitten by the enemy. Someone who has been bruised or battered, who's been wounded on the inside. I made so many connections between the natural and the spiritual as my hand was healing that year.

I noticed the first thing the snakebite did was take out my nervous system. I felt no pain, but it also made me disoriented! I couldn't think clearly. That is what the enemy does when he comes at us. He's very sneaky. We go numb and do not feel what's really happening. We shut down and go into shock. Our spirits react the way my natural nervous system was reacting. That is what happened to me when I was in college and the enemy tried to take me out.

I also noticed that what was going on in my hand was not registering in my brain. It's like they were two separate things. I realized for the body of Christ to work as it should, the head has to communicate with the hand. There was kind of a disconnect there for a while, and I realized that's what the enemy does. He keeps us broken and disconnected from any form of reasoning. All the bruising, all the colors, all the swelling, are just pictures of what the abuser does.

But where the enemy comes to kill, steal, and destroy, Jesus came to give us life and life more abundantly. This we must never forget!

During the healing process, I went to Pensacola many times with several friends. Revival had hit, and we went, chasing the presence of God. On one trip, I heard that Rodney Howard Brown was in another part of town. He was known for the miraculous, and people getting healed in his services. I was going to show him my hand and watch God supernaturally put it back together! That was my plan anyway.

At the beginning of the service, he started throwing materials into the audience. He said, "Who wants a book, raise your hand! Who wants a VHS tape, raise your hand! Who wants this book, raise your hand!"

I wasn't interested in any of that. I wanted healing, so I was just sitting in my chair. I wasn't standing up, jumping, raising my hands, and screaming like many people. I was watching, but I was just waiting to get to the healing part. He picked up one of those VHS tapes and he hurled it through the air. That thing went over the heads of hundreds of people and landed right square in my lap. I looked down at it and read, *Joseph and His Coat of Many Colors.*

"I don't want this!" I thought. "I want healing! I want that man to lay his hands on me!" But all I got was a tape.

Finally, he began to preach. The Anointing was strong. At the end of the evening, they had to bring him out the backdoor because we were in a tent. He passed fairly close to me, and people were trying to touch him as he walked by. I was only about six feet from him.

"If I can just push through the crowd," I thought, "if I could just touch him, maybe what he's carrying will come into my body and I'll be healed."

I watched as he touched people and they fell under the power of God. I was fighting to get over bodies, pushing forward and stepping over people. When I got to the door, he looked at me and said, "What do you want, sister?"

I showed him my hand. "I got bit by a snake."

He looked into my eyes and then he touched me with his elbow and said, "Take it, sister!"

I didn't understand what he was doing. *That's it? "Take it sister"!? That's what I get after all this waiting to be healed?* But I said out loud, "Okay God, I'll take whatever You have."

The minute I accepted it, the minute I yielded and received it, I felt the strength of God go into my body. I fell down right there in the threshold of that door. People had to step over me to get out!

I wasn't sure what was going on, but I knew I wanted whatever God had and I was going to lie there until my body absorbed it all. So that's what I did. I lay there. Someone came along and pulled me over to the side and several of my friends stood around me so I wouldn't get stepped on. When I finally got up, my hand didn't look any different, but I knew God had made a deposit in my life. I was thinking God was going to heal my hand, but He had other plans.

Months later, I was cleaning my living room and found that VHS tape. I stuck it in and began to listen about Joseph and his coat of many colors. Rodney Howard Brown explained that the colors represented different anointings Joseph carried. He taught about everything Joseph had. He said there are people walking around with a mantle like Joseph's who have lots of different anointings. People who can lead worship, preach, and teach. People who lay hands on the sick.

God was talking to me through the VHS tape I'd been so frustrated about! He wanted me to move in many arenas of ministry. I'd been asking the Lord what He really wanted me to do. "Do you want me to lead worship? I'll be a worship leader. Do you want me to disciple people? I'll do that. Do you want me to pray for the sick? I'll do that. Whatever it is you want God, just show me which one!"

God had called me to do Kingdom work, and all of those things would be necessary. He would give me everything I needed for the life He called me to. I sat and listened, and rewound some parts over and over again, trying to soak it all in. God had given Joseph an apostolic anointing and He wanted me to accept that. He wanted me to take the mantle that He had chosen for me. Many colors represented many facets, but also seemed to bring many misunderstandings.

The entire year, I knew God was going to restore my hand. I knew He was doing a deeper work and the entire snake bite was a picture of what He was doing in my life. Time passed and my hand healed. And from then on, I knew God had anointed my hands for war and my fingers for battle. I knew I could trust what God said, and not what things looked like in the natural.

The Occult

I have explained what the Lord revealed to me about the Gates of Hell and legal entrances and access points the enemy can gain in our souls if we open the gates of lies, sin, iniquity or trauma. But over the years, I discovered some things about ministering to anyone who has come in contact with satanic worship or the occult. This can be as innocent as reading a horoscope, playing with a ouija board, calling for Bloody Mary, visiting a curandero or witch doctor, or full-on cooperating and making covenants with the Kingdom of Darkness. When a person comes into agreement with the occult, the enemy of the soul can walk right in through any gate.

Often times, if I am ministering to people who have had casual contact with the occult and may not have even realized it, we will get to the core and I will ask them what they see, hear, or feel. If they are unable to sense anything at the core, they may say something like, "I just see black," or, "There's nothing there." When this happens, I have learned to ask about the occult. Agreement with the kingdom of darkness has a way of creating a block in our souls. It is like running into a brick wall during ministry. Nothing gets in and nothing gets out until the block is removed.

Whenever I find the occult in a person's life, I first have the person repent of his or her involvement in that practice. I have the person forgive anyone who brought the occult into his or her life, and I have them completely renounce all occult activity. And then we ask forgiveness for making any agreements with darkness.

Years ago, we took a ministry team to Russia. One morning, I ministered to a young man from Nigeria who was in his final year of Medical School. He had received Jesus after arriving in Russia and had been a Christian for three years. Even though his life had completely changed since receiving Jesus, he knew he still wasn't free. He had not been able to break through certain patterns in his life.

We prayed through his life together, forgiving things, asking forgiveness, and looking for access points for the enemy. He shared that his mother, and his grandmother before her, were witchdoctors. As a child, he was taken to a witchdoctor and given a potion to drink. He told me it made his belly swell and that after that day he was able to tell the future. From the time he was six years old. his parents had used him to make money as a fortune-teller. He was a child, of course, and not in charge of his own choices, but an agreement was made with the occult to give him power to use, and he was used as an agent for the Kingdom of Darkness.

Now, as an adult, he was in his last semester of medical school. He had met Jesus and gotten saved two or three years prior, but hadn't been able to get rid of demons taunting him. Because he grew up under witchcraft, he understood the demonic realm, but did not know how to get free.

After he finished telling me his story, we took the precious blood of Jesus and applied it to his heart and his life. We forgave his family for generations of witchcraft. He felt it break off his life and leave his body. He knew that he now had the power to break those sinful patterns off his life. He knew he was free.

Here is the really cool part! Later that afternoon he called his brother in Nigeria to tell him what God had done.

"That explains what's happened to Mom," the brother said. "She's been different all day and I didn't know what was happening to her." When he forgave the generations of witchcraft in the bloodlines of his family, his mother was freed of the iniquity that had been passed down to her as well! We prayed in Russia, and her life was impacted in Africa!

I began to understand at another level the Blood of Jesus that has been given to the Church. *If we forgive anyone their sin, it is forgiven*! Even if that person is on the other side of the planet. How amazing is our God! Breaking the power of generational sin or iniquity in our lives is the beginning of true transformation.

———

A friend invited me to her home to hear a traveling prophet speak. As he was teaching, he asked if anyone wanted to receive the baptism of the Holy Spirit. Hands went up all over the house. My friend asked me to pray with some of the people to be touched by the Holy Spirit.

As I laid my hands on the first woman, I sensed a demonic block to her ability to receive. This woman didn't speak English, and so her husband was with her, translating in Spanish. At least that is what I assumed. I asked her husband if she had ever been involved in occult activity. Through him she told me that when she was a child her parents used curanderos for healing. They would rub an egg on her, take her to witchdoctors, and use other practices typical in the Mexican culture that many do not even realize are rooted in witchcraft.

I asked her to repent and forgive her parents in order to remove the demonic block. As soon as she prayed and forgave the witchcraft, she began to laugh and cry and jump up and down. I asked her husband what was going on, and he told me that God had just opened her ears. Literally! I hadn't realized it, but she had been deaf for years. Her husband was translating to Spanish, not because she could hear him in Spanish, but she could read lips in Spanish. When we removed the demons, her hearing was completely restored! I prayed as the Lord directed, not knowing what He was doing in her life.

Many of the supernatural events I have experienced have happened just this way. The Bible says, "And these signs will follow those who believe." I did not even have to understand what was going on for God to show his power. I might not lean so heavily on Him for everything if I knew what was coming or what to do. That is exactly where God wants us.

Stories

Linda was suffering from kidney trouble. Her doctors told her, "Your kidneys are barely functioning and you're not going to live another week if you don't start dialysis."

"The Lord didn't tell me that, and I'm not going to do it. Thank you," said Linda. Her friends and family all thought she was crazy and told her she was going to die.

"No, I'm not. I'm going to live and declare the goodness of God!"

At the time I am writing this, that was seven years ago! Her husband makes her go to the doctor on a regular basis. Every time they do blood work they tell her, "Your blood is very bad. You're going to die unless you go on dialysis!"

And every time she tells them, "No I'm not going to die! I'm not done yet."

They told her to go home and get on hospice care. She called me and said, "Okay, they put me on hospice care. What do I do?"

"You need to pray through everything God shows you. You need to Shalom yourself every day and every night until you've found every gate of access the enemy has to your health."

That woman is still walking and still smiling. She comes to every workshop we put on. It's amazing! The same power that raised Christ from the dead lives in us, and Linda grabbed on to that truth! She believed the Bible says she can choose life, so she chose life. She didn't, and still doesn't, care what her kidneys are saying. She tells her kidneys every day, 'Kidneys, live and be healed!" She is choosing to believe the truth that she can live and refuses to believe the statistics about her kidneys. She went to God, and He told her to choose life.

One day two women showed up for ministry. They'd driven several hours together to have back-to-back sessions. The first lady was with me for two and a half hours. In her session, we prayed through sixty years of trauma, lies, iniquity and sin. Her hardest years were in her thirties when her husband had a mistress for five years. She felt trapped in the marriage and wanted to leave, but didn't want her small children to have divorced parents. Her husband eventually gave up the other woman and became a wonderful spouse to her. But after twenty-five years, she knew they had never regained the intimacy and trust that had been lost. We prayed through this, and she was finally able to forgive him for the affair and open her heart and her body to intimacy with him. They have a wonderful marriage today!

The second woman came in for her session and we went through another sixty years in two and a half hours. When we came down the stairs the first woman was waiting for us at the bottom of the stairs. Her eyes were full of light, and she was so excited that she could hardly get her words out. She was literally bouncing for joy. We asked her to share her excitement with us.

She told us that she was a diabetic and had been on three insulin shots a day since she was in her thirties. After her session she'd gone downstairs to check her blood sugar and it was normal, even though she was overdue for her next shot. She thought that the machine must be broken. She checked again on a back-up machine that she kept in her purse. That didn't give her the reading she expected either, so she got a third one from her car. Having checked and re-checked on three different machines every half-hour for two and a half hours while I was in a session with her friend, she finally realized she didn't need insulin any longer. God had healed her and she was no longer diabetic!

I had spent over two and a half hours listening to her life story, but she made no mention of diabetes, high blood pressure or medication. We talked mostly about her marriage and emotional trauma. We prayed for the damage to her soul to be healed. We prayed through the memories and emotions from her childhood, and from her husband's affair. We prayed for the light of Jesus, the Son of Righteousness, to invade every area of her heart. I did not lay hands on her, and I did not ask God for physical healing, because she never told me she was sick! We prayed for the God Who is holy and whole to make her holy and whole, and that was exactly what He did!

God healed her, soul and body; He didn't need me to know what was going on. He wants us healed AND He wants us whole.

> *Beloved, I pray that you may prosper in all things and be in health, just as your soul prospers (3 John 2, NKJV).*

So, if the Son sets you free, you will indeed be free (John 8:36, TLB).

———⁓◦◦⌒◦◦⌒◦◦⁓———

I ministered to a man in his fifties who told me he had Asperger's syndrome. He weighed eleven pounds at birth and was his mom's first baby. His mother was hospitalized for days, so his grandmother had taken him home. She thought that since he was a big baby, he should have twice as much formula. His little tummy wasn't ready for that much milk and he screamed in pain. So, he was called a "bad baby," a "hard baby," who cried all the time. And every year on his birthday, he was reminded that he had nearly killed his mother at birth. This was so painful for him to hear that he didn't want to have birthdays.

He was a brilliant child, but couldn't sit still in school. It wasn't long before the teacher moved him to the special needs class. He could do his work perfectly, but had a hard time sitting still, so his entire education was spent separated from other children. He was told horrible things about himself and began to believe there was something wrong with him. The other children were cruel to him.

We prayed through the trauma of his birth and all the things he had shared with me. At the end of the prayer session, I opened my eyes and he was swinging his head back and forth as hard as he could. When I asked if he was okay, he said this was the first time in his life he wasn't in pain. All the memories from his birth had been stored in the muscles of his neck and shoulders. The pressure of his delivery had broken his collar bone, and his little head and shoulders held all that pain. No wonder he couldn't sit still as a small child! He didn't know why he was hurting, he just knew he was. Now, after praying, all the pain had left his body.

Was he healed of Asperger's? Did he have autism, or was it a child trying to cope with pain? Whatever it was, it was gone now. Only God knows for sure what led to the diagnosis he had come to believe was his identity. We prayed for a fresh start and a new identity as a son of God, healed and whole! This was a mystery, and the Bible says God delights in revealing mysteries to the ones He can trust.

———∿∿⚬⚬ℯ↻⚬↻ℯ⚬⚬∿∿———

One afternoon, I was praying with a woman diagnosed with fibromyalgia. I asked where her pain was. She said it began with pressure in her upper arms, but then moved all over her body. She was in constant pain. As soon as she said the words "upper arms," I had an image of a man squeezing her arms and pushing her against a wall. I asked if she had ever been physically abused. She said that twenty years before, she had been in a relationship with an angry man who would grab her arms, hold her against a wall and scream in her face. "But that was years ago," she said. She explained that she escaped that abusive relationship and had now been in a healthy marriage for several years.

The Lord told me she still held the trauma of that relationship in the muscle tissue of her arms, so we asked Jesus to arise with healing in His wings and shine His light into every fiber of her body. She forgave her abuser, and as Jesus healed the muscle memory, the pain left her body completely. Fibromyalgia was completely healed!

Carrying traumatic memories in our bodies often causes us to make decisions based on fear. Once healed, decisions made from a place of wholeness lead us to a greater level of wisdom. Let's invite the Son of Righteousness into these past experiences, and let the Light of His glory heal our memories and restore damaged tissue.

But unto you who revere and worshipfully fear My
name shall the Sun of Righteousness arise with heal-

ing in His wings and His beams, and you shall go
forth and gambol like calves [released] from the stall
and leap for joy, (Malachi 4:2, AMPC).

—⁓⦿⟡⦿⟡⦿⁓—

One day a girl from Texas State University showed up to my house and told me someone had told her she should come. I invited her in and asked her what she needed.

She looked at me and asked, "Who are you?"

"My name is Monte. What's going on and how may I help you?"

She had shared with a friend that she heard voices in her head and the friend said, "You need to go see this lady, Monte." When she heard my name, the voices reacted strongly, yelling at her, saying that she could not go see "that lady." She began to tremble inside. She didn't understand what was happening, but she knew if the voices were telling her *not* to come, then she should probably do the exact opposite!

I was shocked, but heard the Lord say, *The demons know who you are.* God began to teach me that I also needed to know exactly who I was, grounding my identity in the King of Heaven.

> *And Jesus healed many who had various diseases.*
> *He also drove out many demons, but He would not*
> *let the demons speak because they knew who He was*
> *(Mark 1:34, NIV).*

> *When Jesus had called the Twelve together, He gave*
> *them power and authority to drive out all demons*
> *and to cure diseases, and He sent them out to pro-*

claim the Kingdom of God and heal the sick (Luke 9:1; 2, NIV).

On another occasion, I met with a woman from San Antonio who had heard about me and wanted to see me. As we sat in the living room, I quickly realized she was so paranoid that she couldn't put words together that made any sense. I asked if I could pray for her and she submitted to prayer. I asked God to bring me the part of her that could tell me what was going on inside of her. Immediately, I felt the room shift and knew there was a "spirit" in the room. It didn't feel like any demon I had ever sensed. It felt holy, but I also knew it wasn't the Holy Spirit.

Who are you? I asked.

My name is Magdala. I am her guardian.

In that instant, my mind went back to a memory from many years earlier. It was one afternoon when I was talking to Dr. Joe Albright, that wonderful minister and teacher from Houston who was teaching me how to bring healing to the very broken. I remembered him saying, "Every once in a great while, you will come across someone who is so broken that they cannot speak, and the Lord will allow their guardian angel to tell you their story."

I knew that this spirit was an angel. I had heard and felt plenty of demonic spirits, but this was my first time hearing from an angel, and my whole world shifted. I had a guardian angel talking to me in my living room!

The angel told me she had been trying to get this woman to see me for over a year. She knew God would heal her if she could get her to my house. She told me all the things I needed to know in order to pray effectively for this woman. She had nearly been killed in a sexual attack by a relative when she was five years old. She had never fully recovered, and for most of her life she had been unable to think clearly. She had never been mentally or emotionally stable, and spent most of her adult life moving in and out of various institutions. After we prayed together, though, she was finally at peace, with a sound mind. Magdala thanked me. The woman left, completely changed. I was changed, too. I knew that not only did demons know my name, but the angels did, too! Our God is so cool and is able to do so many amazing things!

> *Never doubt God's mighty power to work in you and accomplish all this. He will achieve infinitely more than your greatest request, your most unbeliev-able dream, and exceed your wildest imagination! He will outdo them all, for His miraculous power constantly energizes you (Ephesians 3:20, TPT).*

One evening a woman walked into our Bible Study group. "Will you pray for my sister?" she asked. "She's in a coma and the doctors have given her only three days to live."

"Of course I will," I answered. "Where is she? What happened to her?"

No one knew exactly, but Audra's sister had apparently called 911, and when the paramedics arrived at her home, they found her unconscious, Audra explained. She had been in a coma for two weeks. The doctors didn't know what to do with her. No medications were working and her body was shutting down. "They told me she only has days to live," Audra said.

The next day, my friend Anita and I drove to Austin with a vanload of our kids. We were both stay-at-home moms with eight children between us. Anita was telling me how bad this woman's condition was and, over all the noise of the kids, I tried to pray and hear God. I leaned into the window, closed my eyes and asked the Lord what He wanted me to do.

He said, *Tell her, "You're going to be okay. You can wake up now."* I felt the Lord's peace, and knew it was His voice.

When we arrived at the hospital, Anita took the kids to the waiting room and I went through the double doors into ICU when I realized I didn't even know the woman's name! I started looking into different rooms for her. "Who are you?" a nurse asked. "What are you doing here?"

"I'm here to pray for my friend's sister," I said.

"What's her name?" the nurse asked.

"I don't know."

"You don't know her name?" the nurse asked incredulously. "You're going to have to leave!" she ordered.

Just then a woman stepped out of a room. "Are you Monte?" she asked. I nodded. "Anne's in here. Come in."

"You can't just walk into an Intensive Care Unit like that!" the nurse called out as I quickly stepped into the room.

Anne's face was terribly swollen and there were tubes everywhere, draining fluid out of her body. She looked close to death. The stench in the room was overpowering. My heart went out to her mother, who had been in the room for days, watching her child die. I asked her if I could pray for her.

"No!" she said. "You pray for my daughter!"

Because of the stench, I really didn't want to get any closer, but I stepped toward the bed. The atmosphere was so foul and dark that I couldn't think straight. As I stepped closer, I could see green fluid coming out of her mouth and nose. I didn't know what to say. I put my hand on her, closed my eyes and began to pray very quietly in tongues. The enemy started to back off, and I became more peaceful.

Then my mind became crystal clear and I remembered what the Lord had told me in the van. I leaned in and whispered, very quietly, so no one else could hear me, "Jesus sent me to tell you, you're going to be okay. You can wake up now."

As I turned to leave, I touched Anne's foot and said, "I'll come back in a few days and when I do, you'll be sitting up." Suddenly she began to move and her eyes opened. She blinked a few times. At that moment the nurse came in.

"She moved!" I shouted. "I think she's waking up!"

"Oh no," the nurse said, waving me away, "it's just nerves." She looked at Anne and asked, "Can you hear me?" Anne blinked rapidly. The nurse pulled the tube out of her mouth. Anne tried to speak but only made a gurgling sound, and I couldn't make out any words. She nodded her head and tried to smile. The surprised nurse said the tube may have affected her speech, but it should heal.

Right before I left, Anne opened her eyes and I told her again, "When I come back, you'll be sitting up." I left her with a very excited mom and a very shocked nurse! A week later I went back to the hospital. Anne was in a different room, sitting up in a wheelchair.

"I've been waiting for you," she said.

I knelt beside her chair and said, "You look so much better! Is there anything I can do for you?"

"Yes, I want to know Jesus," she said.

I led her in a prayer and she gave her heart to Jesus. She then told us her side of the story. She had been bathing her dog in the woods behind her house and suddenly felt something come over her. She felt dizzy and everything went dark. Feeling dazed and confused she managed to get back to the house and call 911. She passed out, and didn't remember anything until she felt her body wake up in the hospital.

It was a few years before I saw her again at our Bible Study. I didn't recognize her at first, and she had to tell me where we had met! She was doing well and had gotten married. She was so thankful for what God had done, and had been walking with the Lord ever since.

I don't pretend to understand everything that happened. What I do understand though, is that God kept her alive long enough to get her help and healing so she could spend the rest of her life in relationship with Him.

Quite some time after this I got a phone call.

"Do you still cast out demons?" a voice on the other end asked. "My husband and I are pastors in a small town in Texas. This summer at Bible School we led a ten-year-old girl to the Lord and she asked us to pray for her mother. When we went to the house and knocked on the door her mother started screaming, "Unclean! Unclean! You have to leave me! I'm unclean!" We don't know what to do. Can you help us?"

"Does she want to be healed?" I asked.

"Yes, but we don't know how. Could you come?"

"Of course, I'll come," I told them, and we set the date to go to her little church.

When my friend Kay and I arrived, there was a long line of people wanting prayer. We were given a room where we prayed for people, one by one, all day long. The first one to come was the mother of the young girl… the "unclean" woman. This poor woman had lived in this small town her entire life and had no real friends. She walked the streets of town, mumbling. Her mother had abused her, beating her and throwing things at her. The one thing her mother had liked about her was her hair, and the only time the mother touched her in a nice way was when she was brushing her hair. Sadly, as a hurting child she started to pull her hair out to get back at her mom. She continued pulling it and could not stop doing it even after her mother had died. For most of her life, she had no hair at all.

We prayed and separated the demons from her, and Jesus came into that place in her heart; she was able to forgive her mother and all the abuse of her childhood. She was free, and she left peaceful, calm, and in her right mind.

Several months later, Robin Mark, a well-known Christian singer, came to our church to give a concert. People came from all over and this woman was one of them. I was helping to get things ready for the concert when she came up to me.

"Do you remember me?" she asked. She looked familiar, but I couldn't place her. "The last time you saw me I didn't have any hair!" Then I remembered her! She now had beautiful brown curls all over her head, and her face was full of light. Jesus had given her back her life, and her hair!

A few weeks later I preached at her church on a Sunday morning and she was the official greeter! A woman who had felt so unclean that she couldn't open her front door was now opening the door of the House of God to everyone. The woman everyone had known as the "town crazy" had become the town evangelist and was leading people to the Lord through her testimony!

One day in June, another woman called. "I have an appointment with you in October," she said, but my doctor said I won't be alive in October. Could you see me sooner?" I asked her what was going on. "I died three times in May, and they brought me back. They don't know what's going on. They just know I keep dying!"

I worked her into my schedule as early as possible. She was a tall woman, but she probably weighed only ninety pounds. She looked like death, which was not surprising since she had died three times, and three times they had shocked her and brought her back. She was young, only fifty.

She sat in front of me and I asked, "Do you want to die? Because, you know, as a man thinketh, so he is. So, do you want to die?"

"No, I don't want to die! We just retired and bought an RV. We're planning to go on road trips to places we've wanted to see for a long time."

"How's your marriage?" I asked.

"Oh, we have a great marriage. All our kids are finally grown. We get along great."

"How are your finances?"

"We're good. We just retired. We've been waiting for this time. But now all this is happening, and I have no clue why."

It was a fascinating session. I learned that the first time she died was from a bad reaction to a medication. She had apparently overdosed. They brought her back, and got her medications balanced out, but she died again. The doctors told her, "We don't know why you died this time, but we're going to monitor you very closely." She lived another week and then coded again.

That's when her doctor told her, "You are healthy; there's no apparent reason for this. If you know anyone in spiritual healing, you should look into that. There's nothing more that we can do."

So she came to me and Jesus revealed to me that when she died the first time, her brain, and her memory, registered her as dead. The brain can live up to ten minutes after the heart stops beating, and it can continue to store memory during that time. She went through the trauma of dying, and when the paramedics who revived her first acknowledged that she was dead, her brain recorded it.

A week or two later, the memory popped up. "She's dead." Well, if you're dead, you don't need your heart to beat. You don't need your blood to pump. You don't need your lungs to work. Her body responded to the brain's memory of death and everything else stopped functioning.

If you have been with people who are dying, you've seen this process at work. Once a person knows he is dying, he becomes more peaceful. The soul agrees and then the body says, "Okay, we're dying. Start shutting down." The body's remaining energy goes to the heart, lungs and brain. You need to breathe and keep your heart beating, and you want to think. Her brain was saying she was dead and giving the signal to her body not to bother with any other functions.

Death was recorded in her brain, not once, but three times. So we went to all three events and invited the Son of Righteousness to arise in her and heal her memories. We prayed the Scripture from Malachi and released the light of Jesus into her brain, into the hospital room and into her doctor. She forgave the medications and the overdose. She forgave the doctor. She forgave everything. And she didn't die anymore. The same power that raised Christ from the dead lives in you and me. How awesome is that?

> *But unto you who revere and worshipfully fear My name shall the Sun of Righteousness arise with healing in His wings and His beams (Malachi 4:2, AMPC).*

> *But if the Spirit of Him who raised Jesus from the dead dwells in you, He who raised Christ Jesus from the dead will also give life to your mortal bodies through His Spirit, Who dwells in you (Romans 8:11, NASB).*

I talked to her a few days later and she said she was feeling much better and had more energy. "But," she said, "I'm just not interested in eating the stuff they tell me to eat."

"What are they giving you to eat?"

"It's some nasty powdery green stuff. I don't know what it is."

"No one wants to eat that! Why don't you eat something that tastes good? How about a cheeseburger?" I asked.

"Can I have a cheeseburger?"

"Why not?" I asked. "You're not dying!"

So, she started eating what she wanted and got her appetite and her strength back. I learned from this how powerful our thoughts can be, and that we can restore even our memories through the healing light of Jesus.

Next Level

Beth Shalom has been a full-time ministry for years now. I never set out to do this. I just asked God to teach me how to free and heal the people who were in front of me. I never imagined He would show me so much. Over the years, it became impossible for me to see and pray for everyone who reached out, and my friends and prayer warriors began to ask me to teach them the things God had taught me.

Today, many people have been trained in all that God has taught me over the years, and they do ministry sessions in their own cities, in their own homes. Many of us have traveled together internationally to take the ministry to many nations. People hear of us, hear a testimony from someone they know who was healed or delivered by Jesus through Beth Shalom, and they fly in from all over the country to receive sessions.

One morning, a young woman came to us from Maryland. My husband Hugh did her session and, afterward, the three of us went to lunch. I was curious and asked her how she found out about it.

A woman in her church had given her one of our CDs. She listened to it and booked a flight to Austin. I questioned her. "You just heard one CD and decided you would come here?"

"Oh yes. I realized I could get healed for the price of a plane ticket! I found you and booked my flight." I was amazed at her faith, and I knew she was healed.

God has continued to flood our home and our lives with those He wants to heal, and those He wants us to train. He gave us authority to make disciples who can bind up the broken-hearted, set the captives free and heal all disease. We have equipped and ordained over fifty men and women who help us with our mission of bringing wholeness and freedom. In this final chapter, I want to share a few stories of those who are doing Beth Shalom ministry in other regions of the United States. I want you to know that this is not a ministry or a set of tools God has released only to me. There is nothing magic or special about me, except that I have made it my life's mission to say *yes* to the Lord. He uses any size "yes" from any individual who loves Him and will say "yes" to Him.

> *Then Jesus came to them and said, "All authority in heaven and on earth has been given to Me. Therefore, go and make disciples of all nations, baptizing them in the name of the Father and of the Son and of the Holy Spirit, and teaching them to obey everything I have commanded you. And surely, I am with you always, to the very end of the age"* (Matthew 28:18-20, NIV).

A minister in Dallas, Jill, was praying for a young woman in her twenties. The woman had scoliosis and was in constant pain. She was scheduled for surgery, and was scared. She asked Jill to pray with her about her fear of the surgery. Jill asked her when she first remembered her back hurting.

The woman said, "Sixth grade was so hard for me. I had always made straight A's. They put me in gifted classes and really pushed me hard. They gave me a lot of books. There was one teacher who was particularly hard on me. I'd carry all those books in my backpack. I studied so hard, and I always had that heavy backpack with me, and my back hurt all the time."

Jill began to pray for this woman. She prayed about this little sixth grader with the heavy backpack and the mean teacher. She forgave the teacher for being so hard on her and putting her under so much pressure. She forgave the heavy load of books she had to carry everywhere. She forgave herself for carrying too much weight and for subjecting herself to all of the pressure. As they prayed, the bones and connective tissue in her back started to move. The memories were healed, the muscles began to relax, and her back realigned. The pain instantly left her back. God had healed her and set her free from pain. She came to Jill to pray through the fear of surgery, and it ended up she didn't even need surgery! Her scoliosis was gone after fifteen years!

———— ∽∾∾⸙⊙⸙∾∾ ————

While teaching a workshop in Atlanta, Georgia, I met a woman who had reached the end of her rope. Just days before, she had gone to a bridge, ready to jump off, when she heard God say, *Don't jump. Call Tina.*

She called her friend Tina and told her the story. Tina invited her to an upcoming Beth Shalom workshop. At the workshop, the woman found hope and made an appointment to meet with Betty, one of our ministers in Atlanta. Her marriage was falling apart and she believed it was her fault. Betty walked through her session and

God brought hope and healing into her life. Betty's husband, Tom, ministered to her husband, and they were able to heal their marriage. At the end of her session, Betty asked if there was anything else she wanted to pray about. She told Betty she wanted another child, but had been told that she would never conceive again.

Betty later told me, "I began to pray for her and out of my mouth came the words, 'You will have a little girl!'" Betty was worried. "I can't believe I said that. It just flew out. What if I was wrong?"

But one year later, I returned to Atlanta for a conference. The woman walked in, seven months pregnant, and had just found out that the baby was a girl! Betty had heard from God, and Beth Shalom blessed another family with hope, healing and wholeness!

During a conference in Moss Bluff, Louisiana, a woman spoke to me through her tears and said, "I want to thank you!" I had never met her and I asked why she was thanking me.

This woman had taken her son to the doctor because he was suffering under mental turmoil and suicidal thoughts. As it happened, her doctor, Dr. Jay, was trained in Beth Shalom. He and his wife later ministered to her, her husband and son, and all three were healed. For the first time, her family was whole and she had the Christian home she had always hoped for.

Through tears, she said to me, "Thank you so much for Beth Shalom." What a joy to know this ministry goes out to places and people I could never get to myself, bringing hope and power and love and healing!

Let's get this world healed! Jesus has made a way for us to bring healing to every traumatic situation. Let's open the gates that the King of Glory may come in. Let's turn those Gates of Hell into Gates of Glory! Rise and shine, Church. The Lord has come, and the glory of the Lord is upon you!

> *Lift up your heads, O ye gates; and be ye lifted up, ye everlasting doors; and the King of glory shall come in. Who is this King of glory? The Lord strong and mighty, the Lord mighty in battle. Lift up your heads, O ye gates; even lift them up, ye everlasting doors; and the King of glory shall come in. Who is this King of glory? The Lord of hosts, he is the King of glory (Psalm 24:7-10, KJV).*

> *Arise, shine, for your light has come and the glory of the Lord rises upon you, (Isaiah 60:1, NIV).*

This is the time for the children of God to become the Church victorious. Earth itself is quaking in pain, crying out for us! We must understand the heart of God, and be alert to hear what He's saying and see what He's doing. We must take down the lies that keep us from becoming who God intended us to be, and exercise the power that is ours through the death of Christ.

> *The entire universe is standing on tiptoe, yearning to see the unveiling of God's glorious sons and daughters! (Romans 8:19, TPT).*

My Treasures

I felt like I should begin and end this book with this verse:

> *I will give you hidden treasures, riches stored in*
> *secret places, so that you may know that I am the*
> *Lord, the God of Israel, who summons you by name*
> *(Isaiah 45:3, NIV).*

People have been telling me for years that I need to write a book. *Well who in the world would read it?* I thought. My grandchildren, I supposed, and my friends, and maybe a few people who have been ministered to by Beth Shalom. But along the way, over and over again, people have said to me, "Everyone needs this, Monte."

So here it is. Here are my treasures. My stories. The story of how the God of my life, the God of Israel, summoned me by name. He told me who I am in Him, and what I carry because He gave it to me. He gave me a deep desire for the riches stored in secret places. And now, I am a very rich woman.

I see the supernatural power of God every day of my life. Now, when I see someone broken and hurting on the street, I am not like that three-year-old girl I used to be who hurt for people, but didn't know what to do. I have the keys to the Kingdom, and it is the greatest privilege of my life to use them.

Beth Shalom has gone all over the world and is now available in several states. We see people in our home every week, and when people call from distant places, we refer them to those we've trained and equipped. It's very exciting to hear the stories of Beth Shalom that come from far and wide.

Thank you, Jesus, for sharing your heart with your Church. I pray that we do everything we can to see the Kingdom of God come on Earth, just as it is in Heaven! And Just like Jesus, I declare and charge the church to declare:

The Year of the Lord's Favor

The Spirit of the Sovereign Lord is on me, because the Lord has anointed me to proclaim good news to the poor. He has sent me to bind up the brokenhearted, to proclaim freedom for the captives and release from darkness for the prisoners, to proclaim the year of the Lord's favor and the day of vengeance of our God, to comfort all who mourn, and provide for those who grieve in Zion— to bestow on them a crown of beauty instead of ashes, the oil of joy instead of mourning, and a garment of praise instead of a spirit of despair. They will be called oaks of righteousness, a planting of the Lord for the display of his splendor. They will rebuild the ancient ruins   and restore the places long devastated; they will renew the ruined cities that have been devastated for generations.

-Isaiah 61:1-4, NIV

Scripture References

Scripture quotations are taken from the following translations of the Bible. We are grateful to the publishers for their use.
AMPCAmplified Bible, Classic Edition
ESV English Standard Version
KJV King James Version
MSG The Message
NASBNew American Standard Bible
NIV New International Version
NKJVNew King James Version
NLT New Living Translation
TPT The Passion Translation
TLB The Living Bible

Beth Shalom Ministry

If you would like to learn more about Beth Shalom and this powerful ministry of inner healing and deliverance, please go to the website. www.Bethshalomtexas.com

Beth Shalom Conferences

Monte and her husband Hugh travel extensively to teach this powerful work of Beth Shalom and to train others in understanding and doing this ministry.

Audio Downloads

Downloads and jump drives of talks given by Monte are available and can be ordered through the website. CDs of talks can also be ordered.

Order more copies of this book

You can obtain more copies of this book through this website. If you would like to buy 10 books, to give as gifts, or to use as a group training and Bible Study, a discount is available.

Beth Shalom Study Workbooks

There are two study workbooks available entitled, "Freedom Fighters Workshops." These two books provide teaching on the principles that this miraculous work of deep inner healing and deliverance through Jesus Christ is built upon. The books can be ordered through the website, www.bethshalomtexas.com.

The ministry of Beth Shalom has a number of trained ministers in different states. You can find the nearest place to you that a Beth Shalom Minister is available. As of the time of publication, we only have ministers in a few states, but the number of trained ministers is growing, as more people are feeling called by God and are committed to studying how to be more effective in ministry.

Printed in the USA
CPSIA information can be obtained
at www.ICGtesting.com
CBHW040254261023
1419CB00015B/13